MASTERS *of* MARRIAGE

A RELATIONSHIP DEVOTIONAL FOR COUPLES

AN ANTHOLOGY
- IN COLLABORATION WITH -
HEARTLIFE MINISTRIES

MASTERS OF MARRIAGE
A Relationship Devotional for Couples

HeartLife Ministries
Post Office Box 116
Flossmoor, Illinois 60422
www.heartlifetoday.org

Copyright © 2021 Heartlife Ministries
ISBN 978-1-943343-98-0

Designed & Published by
Destined To Publish
www.destinedtopublish.com

We dedicate this book to our brother in Christ,
the late
Patrick B. Owens,
and his beautiful wife, our sister in Christ,
Keteena Owens.

A friendship grew into a DIVINE CONNECTION of the heart. We are forever grateful for this God-ordained relationship. They are our partners in ministry, our friends, and our family. Thank you for being there in our humble beginnings of marriage ministry, for mentoring us and showing us how to operate in excellence.

Although God called Patrick home, Keteena continues to stand and fight for marriages and families. Their ministry has touched couples all over the world.

ACKNOWLEDGEMENTS

We would like to say thank you to every couple who participated in this labor of love to encourage couples around the world. Thank you for your dedication to God and to marriage and the family. We love you and value your willingness to share all that God has placed inside of you.

Wes & Neesha Stringfellow

Joey & Marilyn Alexander

Omarr & Leona Carter

Eric & ArLene Collins Wilson

Michael & Michelle Cooper

Shane & Tracy Dixon

Chris & Nerissa Edden

Chad & Tasha Hart

Jason & Lucinda Hart

Brian & Karin Haysbert

Charles & Meri Horton

Roy & Kimberly Manley

Oliver & Denise Marcelle

Jerry & Chris McQuay

Doug & Shanna Neal

Hasani & Danielle Pettiford

Tony & Ruby Powell

Patrick & Jessica Price

Duane & Tanya Reid

Myion & Ebony Roberts

Mark & Dava Rogers

Dwight & Deidra Roussaw

Jeeva & Sulojana Sam

J. Gregory & Chevelta Smith

Henry & Roz Stuttley

Giovanni & Shamira Tate

Rob & Nicole Wheatley

Chris & Laura White

Marc & Rhonda White

Leon & Tracy Wright

Steven & LaVone Yarbrough

Rodney & Nikeya Young

FOREWORD

What you have in your hands, if it were to be given a value, would be classified as priceless. For what is it worth to you to have a solid, happy marriage that will create a thriving, healthy family, who will glean from what they experience and reproduce the same qualities in their own life?

God spent a great many years investing in His friend Abraham, for He had a plan that Abraham would become the father of many nations. Abraham was not a perfect man; in fact, he had some serious flaws. Yet, what God saw in Abraham was a man who was willing to obey Him. That one attribute enabled him to live a life of faith, which was counted unto him as righteousness.

Believe it or not, God has chosen you, who hold this book in your hand, to walk a journey like Abraham. He has provided you with a tool that contains truths that will bring you and your spouse not only a greater love, but also greater peace, contentment, and joy. These truths can also be transferable to your children, and their children, and so on. Thus, you will, in your own sphere of influence, become a father and mother of many nations.

We all know the attacks that marriages are experiencing. We also know some of the reasons why. Yet knowledge of the "why" is not enough; what we need is the "how" of avoiding or extinguishing those attacks. This book can be your answer. Each contributing couple has highlighted some of the most problematic challenges that every couple faces. Reading one of these short excerpts daily with your spouse will benefit you, and praying together regarding those things that speak to your situation will bring the greatest power source available into you taking the advice and walking them out!

HeartLife Ministries extends a debt of gratitude for the transparency each couple has presented in sharing their testimonies of victory. Gratefully, they have also shared their ministries where you can contact them if you would like to communicate with them further. Take advantage of both the written word and, if needed, the continued expertise of these couples who are learning that marriage does not have to be a life sentence of drudgery but can be a daily adventure of peace, harmony, and satisfying love.

Dr. Alice Maria Crawford

HeartLife Ministries

Dear Couples,

The beauty of marriage we know comes from the Creator God Almighty. God is the one who patterns the body of Christ to marriage.

Marriage isn't just an arrangement; it's an intimate and personal way for us to share the love of God with the world. But the great expectation of having a fairy-tale marriage has a tendency to scare many couples. God did not intend for marriage to be a scary trial in your life. He places in the heart of every human the desire not to be alone. His intention was for two to become one and for a covenant union to be birthed, experiencing the joys of life together.

Although every couple's story starts out differently, many couples enter into their marriage covenant the wrong way, with preconceived notions. We believe there are golden nuggets you can practice along with God's word that can bring a special touch of unity to your marriage.

Over the last 33 years, we have learned that it's the simple things in a marriage that make a difference. The simple practices we have implemented have become staples in our relationship. They keep us connected.

We are excited for you to enjoy this book and use it as a tool on your journey of marriage.

What you learn from the Marriage Masterminds will last a lifetime. You can share the gift of this book with your children and grandchildren, leaving a legacy of beautiful marriages. It is filled with transparency, wisdom, overcoming battles, and golden nuggets to enhance your marriage. The couples who have taken the time to encourage you are truly powerful men and women of God.

> *"Iron sharpeneth iron; so a man sharpeneth the countenance of his friend."* (Proverbs 27:17, KJV)

In a nutshell, it's so important to us that couples make it. It's vital to the next generation. And we don't just want you to make it, but to really embrace and enjoy the journey called marriage.

So, no matter what stage of marriage you are in, embrace the gift of this Marriage Mastermind devotional, and you will welcome a long-lasting marriage and friendship for a lifetime.

Remember, you are never too young or old to start practicing simple ways to keep your marriage healthy. Everyone has something to offer, so be encouraged to start.

Love,

Wes & Neesha

REBOOT YOUR MARRIAGE

W ES & N EESHA

Married ~ September 1988

Why Reboot?

Whenever we hear the word "reboot," we are inclined to think
about our material possessions such as batteries, computers,
and other kinds of technology. But the reboot to which we are
referring is a "reboot" or "repair" in your personal life. No, I'm not
talking about getting rid of your current spouse and upgrading
to a new one; but that *is* a decision many couples are making,
even as you read this page. I am talking about the two of you

deciding, together, to put a fresh surge into your marriage. Too many couples feel that it is impossible for them to find happiness in their marriage. If this is you, you have been lied to by the enemy. God wants better for you. He has better plans for your marriage:

> *"For I know the plans I have for you,"* *says the Lord.*
> *"They are plans for good and not for disaster, to give you*
> *a future and a hope."* (Jeremiah 29:11, NLT)

God spoke to Adam and Eve in the Garden of Eden and told them not to eat from the tree of the knowledge of good and evil, but they chose to believe the lie of the serpent and thought there was a better way. They were deceived, just as people in the world are deceived into believing they cannot have a happy marriage.

When Adam and Eve ate from the forbidden tree, God asked them a question:

> *"And he said, 'Who told you that were naked? Have you*
> *eaten from the tree that I commanded you not to eat*
> *from?'"* (Genesis 3:11, NIV)

Neesha and I like to ask couples, "Who told you that you can't be married and happy too?"

All our lives, we have been fed this lie from various sources that it is impossible to be married and happy. Neesha and I have been interacting with couples for over 15 years, and we've heard this lie and all the rest. The thing we find hardest to understand is how people will take the relationship advice of other people, including famous radio and television hosts, without even considering the fact that the person from whom they are soliciting the advice is not in a healthy relationship him or herself. I once asked a single co-worker who was receiving advice on women from another co-worker, one who had been divorced twice and was single at the time, "Whose advice do you really believe: his or mine?" That does not mean by any stretch of the imagination that people who have been divorced can't give sound advice on relationships, but when you want to understand how something works, isn't it better to go to someone who has figured out how to make it work?

We can make healthy choices that will pay huge dividends. Invest in your marriage by going on retreats and getaways. Get involved in married groups at your church. Neesha and I try to absorb as much knowledge on marriage as possible so that our relationship can stay healthy and enjoyable. That was God's original plan for us. He wanted man to have a companion; He did not just want us to have a roommate for the sake of convenience or "for the good of the children."

Speaking of children, they are watching us; they see and feel everything that is going on in our homes, and it does affect them in one way or another. Every parent who is reading this would likely say that they would lay down their lives for their kids. Well, how about deciding to "*live* for them" instead? I would like to believe that my son, who got married at the age of 23, is looking at my marriage as an example of what a happy marriage looks like. I believe my son knows his marriage will be great because he had a good role model to look up to.

You, too, can find a way to make your marriage a happy one, not only for yourselves, but also for the health and well-being of your children and your children's children. No matter what road you are on, know that God can see you through. He can give you joy in the midst of your journey, no matter what is on your road.

In this book, we will help you discover the tools that will provide strength in your marriage: Self- Repair, Spiritual Examination, Effective Communication, True Intimacy, Financial Freedom, and Investing in Your Marriage.

We are excited that you have joined us and look forward to traveling together on a journey that will lead us to a healthy, successful marriage.

Heartlife Marriage Ministries
www.heartlifetoday.org
info@heartLifeToday.org

Reboot Bootcamp Nuggets

SEAN & MEREDITH FISHER

ERIC & DAWN RANKINS

PATRICK & JESSICA PRICE

KERRY & MICHELLE DAVIS

MICHAEL & MICHELLE COOPER

STEVEN & BRYATTANIE WATSON

TALON & LENI' MCKINNEY

Intent and Interpret

We may have the best intentions when we say something to our spouse, but the most important thing is how they interpret what they hear.

H.A.L.T.

Don't have a conversation when you are feeling:

H: hungry

A: angry

L: lonely

T: tired

- "Make decisions that honor your marriage" (Proverbs 2:6)

- "Keep telling your story"

- "Find the one good thing about each other, especially during bad times."

- "I can see what you don't say."

- "If you ain't a punk in your life, don't be a punk in your spiritual or marital life."

- "When you want to quit, pray harder."

- "Always say you are sorry even if you are not wrong."

- "When you can't figure out what's going on in your marriage… go to the Marriage Creator!"

- "Let's not help the devil; give each other the benefit of the doubt."

- "When you leave God out of your decisions, things will go haywire!"

AN INTIMATE CONVERSATION WITH GOD

O M A R R & L E O N A C A R T E R

Married ~ September 1995

How do you foster emotional intimacy in your marriage? It's a question we've asked ourselves many times. In our upcoming book called *SEXpectations: Strategies to Navigate the Misconceptions of Sex in Marriage to Create Long-Lasting Intimacy*, we outlined our perspective of emotional intimacy.

Her: Emotional

It's incredible how unemotional I thought I was. I consider myself tough-skinned, and before my marriage, I would brush off conflict or hurt feelings and keep going. But when I got married, I had to learn to tune into my emotions more. I realized that I couldn't brush off conflict within my marriage. Through thick and thin, I had to feel connected with my husband. I had to feel like making love to my husband. But in order to connect with my husband sexually, I had to connect with him emotionally long before we got to the bedroom.

In intimate relationships, more often than not, women must be emotionally stimulated before they can be sexually stimulated. I fall into the "more often than not" category. It took me a while to understand that I needed the emotional intimacy to connect with my husband through sexual intimacy. He was the opposite. He needed sexual intimacy to connect with me emotionally. If I'm being honest, I thought we were supposed to be on the same page. I would get offended because he came home so excited to sexually connect when I hadn't talked with him all day.

We implement strategies and techniques now that we understand our differences. It's not wrong how my husband shows up, it's just different from how I show up. One of the things that we implement in our marriage that I share with other couples is taking the time to connect in the kitchen before you connect in the bedroom. Find ways to stimulate your mind emotionally so that sexual stimulation is a continuation of the intimacy you've been fostering all day. It took me years to learn that, so I want to shave the learning curve for you.

His: Emotional

As soon as I walk through the door, I'm ready to go. I'm ready to get physical with my wife. I don't need any warm-up or primer. In the dead of winter, I'm hot and ready to start. In the US Marines, before going in the field, we'd have our rifles in hand, chanting, "Locked, cocked, and ready to rock!" It's a bit extreme, but you get the idea.

When we first got married, it was a little easier riding the waves of emotions after the wedding and honeymoon. How does a date night compete with a wedding night? Yeah, it doesn't. I always joke in my head that I have to do two somersaults, a backflip, and a handstand to get a spark and it still might not start.

For me, it's the physical connection that leads to the emotional connection, which is common for men. When it comes to sex, unlike Whitney Houston, I don't get so emotional, baby. Or do I?

Many times, men release their pent-up emotions through physical intimacy instead of communicating those day-to-day emotions to their spouse. Through that physical connection, men let down their guards, whether it's because of feelings of respect or closeness, vulnerability or tenderness.

It is a lot harder for most of us to lead with emotions. My goal is to do one more backflip; no, just kidding. I try to meet my wife where she is, not where I want her to be. It can start with a gaze, a wink, a peck on her cheek, or a simple "How was your day?" The point is to connect so that we can connect.

Reflection Guide: Emotional
An Intimate Conversation with God

God, show me how to emotionally connect with my spouse in an ongoing way. Please teach me how to express my feelings to my spouse and avoid suppressing my feelings and emotions.

> *"May your fountain be blessed, and may you rejoice in the wife of your youth."* (Proverbs 5:18, NIV)

Rekindle Assignment

Have a conversation with your spouse about the expectations you have for one another and share your feelings. For example, in what ways have you reserved your emotions toward your spouse? What are your expectations for your spouse to express their emotions to you?

COUNTERCULTURE MARRIAGES
www.counterculturemarriages.com

ASKING NON-JUDGMENTAL QUESTIONS

Eʀɪᴄ & AʀLᴇɴᴇ Cᴏʟʟɪɴs Wɪʟsᴏɴ

Married ~ March 2019

Life has a way of teaching your life's lesson along the way, especially when you have reached a certain age and given up on the idea of ever having a relationship where someone truly gets you, knows everything about you without ever wanting to change a thing about you.

This was the case for me and Eric. I knew what I wanted. After several failed marriages, it was time to know ArLene. I was not willing to compromise nor lower my standards just to say I have a man in my life. It took some time to be healed, whole, and complete. I was there and was good with God even if it meant spending the rest of my life single. I come to realize that singleness was not a curse, nor was marriage the cure. (Insert taken from the book *Thrive* by Lina AbuJamra.)

Eric, on the other hand, was at the other end of the spectrum in being comfortable with where he was in life. He had started over after an accident that left him partially blind in one eye, losing everything to start over. He had totally given up on women and made a vow, "I am never getting married again." His journey in life after that decision made him want to know God up close and personal to find Eric.

The weekend of April 6-8, 2018, at a conference in Chicago, our paths crossed, and as they say, "the rest is history." The weeks and months that followed that initial meeting led to many conversations where we had to be transparent and open, especially living over 400 miles apart. It was in those conversations that we had to use what we learned during our singleness to know how to love each other by being intentional about courting God's way from the inside out. I used wisdom to by listening to Eric to understand him, and to let him know that what he had to say was important to me to know him better. Eric asked me non-judgmental questions to understand me based on the answers I gave him, rather than what he expected me to say. We learned that love is actions and not just words. The actions should be a manifestation based on the words confessed to one another.

Trust me, all the work we put in before we got married was well worth the fruit we currently enjoy in our marriage. We had obstacles that came up against us, but we were determined to stick to the plan to do courtship and now marriage God's way.

Choosing God first in our relationship was our way of showing God that we love him and that we respect each other enough to get to know each other personal and up close before making decisions based on physical attraction. This is a decision we never regretted.

In loving each other, we use L.O.V.E. as an acronym in our daily life.

L is learning to listen, to understand, and to respond.

O is to be observant, to see and hear what is not being said that teaches us each other patterns and behaviors.

V is being vulnerable with the change of being hurt, by trusting.

E is for the experience you get about what works and what doesn't so that you can make necessary adjustments, and also the exception of building and having a great relationship.

I STILL DO

Michael & Michelle Cooper

Married ~ October 1991

"Let us not become weary in doing good, for at the proper time we will reap a harvest if we do not give up." (Galatians 6:9, NIV)

Remember your wedding day? Things were fresh and exciting. You and your spouse standing at the altar, vowing to stay together "for better or for worse." Professing before God and man the words "I do." As newlyweds, you created great memories that can last a lifetime. Well, maybe you're now at a point where pain and tears cloud those memories. Despite where you are and what you've been through, know that with God, the path ahead is greater than what you'll leave behind. With the Grace of God, you will forever say "I still do!"

Let's start by defining "still." Typically, we think of "still" as an adjective, meaning "not moving." Perhaps even a noun, "deep silence." However, as you read this and from this moment forth, as it relates to your union, we are encouraging you to think of "still" as an adverb, meaning "ongoing" or "at this present moment."

To say "I STILL DO" is to say that I (we) DO, beyond the very moment we confessed our vows before God. We are continuing to love, cherish, and protect each other. I STILL DO means our love hasn't stopped and will never stop. I STILL DO means that at this present moment, we commit to all that we blissfully agreed to on our wedding day.

We know what you're saying: "Things have changed. He/she doesn't respect or love me anymore. We don't do the things we used to do. It's just not the same." Allow us to encourage you to examine what's different from the day you said "I do" up until now. Who changed? What caused the change? When did the change occur? Where do you see yourself in this change? Why should you accept or reject the change? After 30 years of marriage, we can tell you things will change, people will and should change, and situations and circumstances will change. Change is sometimes needed. After you adjust to the change, you will realize change is sometimes good. However, your love, commitment, dedication, selflessness, and respect should not change.

As we stated, "still" in this case refers to something that is ongoing. So, let's go back and address the 5 W's listed above to help us easily say I STILL DO.

1. **Who changed?** In order to continue to move forward, we must first recognize who stopped moving. We must understand our position in order to control our direction. If one person is not moving in the direction to benefit the union, a change must be made. If both are moving in opposite directions, it is almost impossible to work towards a common goal.

2. **What caused the change?** We must look at why things are different. It may be a number of factors: health, finance, interest, desire, work, etc. Reflect back to when you said "for better or worse, in sickness and health, till death do us part." This is the time to pull on God for strength to carry on together.

3. **When did the change occur?** This isn't as important as you may think. What's key is recognizing and addressing the change. The sooner, the better.

4. **Where do you see yourself in the change?** You must step out of the situation emotionally in order to correct the situation physically. We must realize what part we play in the change process. Are you a change agent or a slave to your circumstances?

5. **Why should I accept or reject the change?** As we all know, change can be good. To accept change does not mean you're weak or you're giving in. It means you recognize that in order to get something different, you must do something different. By rejecting the change, you may be blocking

the opportunity to reach new and higher levels in your union. You can only effectively answer this question after answering the previous four.

"I STILL DO" is simply a choice that you must willingly and actively pursue daily. You must seek God to help you through every good and bad time. Seek Him to guide you through every test and trial. Seek Him to push you beyond what you see so that you may live the life He has prepared for you. Only with Him can you say I STILL DO. He STILL loves you in spite of your flaws. He CONTINUES to forgive you. He CONTINUES to extend grace to you. He will never give up on you. His love for you is ONGOING. For all these reasons, we encourage you to say "I STILL DO."

Couples Committed To Becoming One
Facebook @ C2B1

Priority

Make your spouse your #1 priority.

Your spouse should be number one, over everyone. They should come first – yes, over parents, children, job, church. If you are number one in each other's lives, everything else will simply be just fine. We as couples have a tendency to put everything and everyone else first, but our connection should be stronger than every connection in the human world.

If we are number one in each other's lives, everything else will be accomplished with ease.

John 15:12-14 (NLT)

"This is my commandment: Love each other in the same way I have loved you. There is no greater love than to lay down one's life for one's friends. You are my friends if you do what I command."

Excerpt from SIMPLE SECRETS
Golden Nuggets from God's Word To Enhance your Marriage

TAG, YOU'RE IT!

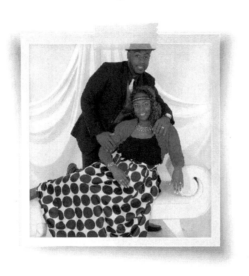

SHANE & TRACY DIXON

Married ~ October 2010

"So I recommend having fun, because there is nothing better for people in this world than to eat, drink, and enjoy life. That way they will experience some happiness along with all the hard work God gives them under the sun." (Ecclesiastes 8:15, NLT)

In 2014 when everything under the sun from PTSD, postpartum, and infidelity hit our marriage, you could not have told the man and woman we were back then that we'd be the husband and wife who are best friends today, on a daily mission to out-love each other.

What happened? Where did we miss the mark? We stopped having fun. We got so caught up in self, life, social media, the kids, and of all the "burdens" of marriage that we totally lost sight of all of the blessings we found in each other. As more and more heartache crept into our home, we pulled farther and farther apart from one another. We went from being spouses to roommates to strangers, and even after we had decided on a whim to really give our marriage another go, we had no idea where to even start.

After 18 months of back and forth with ourselves and God, we made the choice to really put in the work, time, and effort to get us back on track, and after real healing took place in us individually and collectively, we were able to fully work on rebuilding our foundation. At this point we had faith, forgiveness, finances, and even fitness on lock, but the friendship piece was still a little rocky. We knew we loved each other, but did we really still like each other?

So we went back to basics, and incorporated one of our favorite childhood games into our marriage: Tag, You're It! The goal was simple: never stop trying to out-love each other. He focused on giving me his best, and I did the same. We started a pattern of listening to learn, giving grace, and leading with love to rebuild our friendship. We prioritized the priority that was our marriage, and the more we focused on improving our friendship, the more peaceful our home became, the more joyful our children became, and the less stressful work became.

We went from thinking we just didn't have the extra time to spend on each other, to realizing we had been filling up our time to avoid each other. Truth is, once we got the friendship intact, it became easy to find intimacy after infidelity. We went from hell to healed, and fun was a major component in that equation.

No matter what stage you may find yourself in, spice up your marriage by adding some FUN to it. The Bible says that laughter is good for the soul, and no truer words have been spoken. Never stop dating your spouse. Never stop laughing with your spouse. Never stop having fun. When it comes to planning and execution, don't think income, think impact, and don't think funds... think fun!! What are you waiting for? TAG, YOU'RE IT!!

https://linktr.ee/MarriageMiles
MarriageMilesMail@yahoo.com

OUR SECRET WEAPON
TO MARITAL UNITY

B R I A N & K A R I N H A Y S B E R T

Married ~ September 1996

"Submit to one another out of reverence for Christ."
(Ephesians 5:21, NLT)

Let's talk about that wonderful "S" word! If sex came to mind, yes, that can be very unifying too, but we want to talk about submission.

Before you quickly turn the page, please hear us out. We share as a couple who struggled mightily with submission. When we got married in 1996, we were saved, grown folks with our own everything, and like Frank Sinatra, we each wanted to do it "my way." Submission did not come easy.

I, Karin, wrote about this pretty extensively in my book for wives. Today, we want to approach this topic as a couple. What is submission, and why is it our secret weapon to marital unity?

Perhaps you too have heard or experienced the misguided societal viewpoints on submission or how some churches' doctrines have abused it and only directed it towards wives. That is exactly why we referenced Ephesians 5:21. Submission in marriage is mutual. Read that again. It is what both husbands and wives are commanded to do unto God and with each other out of reverence for God.

Let's start with these premises from the Word.

As husbands and wives, we are equal partners in God's gift of life.

Secondly, God does everything in decency and in order. In marriage, God is the head of the man, and then he makes man the head of his wife.

Since husbands are given the Kingdom responsibility for how our marriages and families are run, they also have been given authority. So, if a final decision must be made, as wives, we are called to submit or yield to our husbands' authority.

We are a team, and each spouse has different roles in marriage to complement each other. We each possess skills, gifts, and graces that our spouses do not, and we are expected to bring our whole selves to benefit our union.

Here's the most important part. When we willingly submit to each other, as unto Christ, marriage works. We no longer see submission as merely submitting to each other but as submitting to God. That releases the power behind this decision to willingly be unified.

How do we do that? How do we tap into that glory?

Let me, Brian, share with the husbands first. Brothers, Ephesians 5:25-33 (AMP) makes our submission responsibility crystal clear:

> "Husbands, love your wives [seek the highest good for her and surround her with a caring, unselfish love], just as Christ also loved the church and gave Himself up for her, so that He might sanctify the church, having cleansed her by the washing of water with the word [of God], so that [in turn] He might present the church to Himself in glorious splendor, without spot or wrinkle or any such thing; but that she would be holy [set apart for God] and blameless. Even so husbands should and are morally obligated to love their own wives as [being in a sense] their own bodies. He who loves his own wife loves himself.

> For no one ever hated his own body, but [instead] he nourishes and protects and cherishes it, just as Christ does the church, because we are members (parts) of His body. For this reason a man shall leave his father and his mother and shall be joined [and be faithfully devoted] to his wife, and the two shall become one flesh. This mystery [of two becoming one] is great; but I am speaking with reference to [the relationship of] Christ and the church. However, each man among you [without exception] is to love his wife as his very own self [with behavior worthy

of respect and esteem, always seeking the best for her with an attitude of lovingkindness], and the wife [must see to it] that she respects and delights in her husband [that she notices him and prefers him and treats him with loving concern, treasuring him, honoring him, and holding him dear]."

God tells us to love our wives, to seek their highest good, and to surround them with a caring, unselfish love. We love them sacrificially and lead them spiritually by washing them with the water of God's Word.

We're called to nourish, protect, and cherish our wives as Christ does the church. We prioritize our wives, leaving others and cleaving to our wives by being faithfully devoted to them.

As husbands, without exception, the Word says that we are to love our wives as we do our very own selves, with behavior worthy of respect and esteem and with an attitude of lovingkindness. This submission is not based purely on feelings. It's a decision and an act of our will.

Husbands, ultimately Christ came to serve, not to be served, and to offer himself up for us. That, my brothers, is our role in loving and serving our wives. OUR submission to God in the way that we love our wives causes the two to become one flesh. It releases supernatural unity and power.

I, Karin, will talk to the wives. Sisters, God calls us to submit or to yield to our husband's love and leadership. How do we do that?

The Word tells us to respect and delight in our husbands, notice and prefer them, and treat them with loving concern, treasuring, honoring, and holding them dear. They are to be submitted to and respected unconditionally because of their position, just as we are to be loved unconditionally because of God's command.

It won't be easy, and he won't always get it right, but our trust is in God. We follow our husbands as they follow Christ and encourage them in the ways of God through respect and submission.

So, husbands and wives, are you up for the challenge?

Marriage is most fulfilling in unity. It's a continual process that we intentionally work at, and thankfully, we have the Holy Spirit to empower us to do it.

Talk about it. How can you lovingly submit to each other? What does submission look like in your marriage?

Here's to our marital unity through submission. With God, we've got this!

Queens For Christ
www.karinhaysbert.com
support@karinhaysbert.com

THE LIST

C H A D & T A S H A H A R T

Married ~ September 1996

He had been through a trying relationship, and I had just come out of a horrific divorce. Neither of us were in a hurry to find love again. Chad was putting all of his attention into his work at the Jackson Fire Department. The days were going by, but neither of us had made any serious attempts to make new connections regarding our personal relationships. Then it occurred to Chad after hearing a message at church that maybe he needed to be more specific. He prayed about it and felt God confirmed that being specific was the right next step for now.

Chad grabbed pen and paper and decided to make a list of things that he would want in his next relationship, making sure to start that list with the title "wife." He wanted a wife, and he was encouraged to be very specific about what kind of wife he was looking for. He wrote it all down, beginning with the basics such as wanting his wife to be kind and respectful but very down to earth. He wanted his wife to have a sense of humor and also to be attractive. He specifically mentioned that he preferred his wife to have short hair. He also wouldn't mind if she had some tattoos, just as a reminder she wouldn't be too judgmental. The list was very specific.

Not long after finally settling on the idea that he would pray over the list and be expectant, Chad would meet the woman on the list. A close friend Chad had known since his early teens sent Chad a picture of his sister's new friend. This friend had been seen hanging out with his sister between working two jobs. Chad's friend admitted that his sister's friend wasn't really looking for a new relationship; however, she was single. Chad's friend arranged a meet-up to allow him to meet this woman face to face. When that day came, Chad knew she could be the one. After just one meet-up, Chad was able to check off several of those specifics on his list.

However, Chad wasn't satisfied with just some of the list meeting his expectations. He wanted to spend more time with this woman to determine if she really could be the one. Let me pause and explain the importance of being dissatisfied instead of being discontent. Someone who is discontent will have a tendency to complain about what isn't going right in life. They will find the negatives in any given situation and forget all the good things in life they have already experienced. Discontentment will cause your aspirations in life to come to a standstill. Now, being dissatisfied is the total opposite. Did you know that God doesn't mind if you are dissatisfied? Jeremiah 29:11 tells us that God has a plan for us, and that plan is to prosper us and to continue to give us hope for a future. If we become satisfied with where we currently are, we may never see the full completion of what God has planned.

Not being satisfied or getting too comfortable keeps us seeking after all God has intended for us on our life journey of purpose. Not being satisfied drives us to go after all God has planned, and that is what living a life of purpose is really about: not being satisfied with where you are but being content in the moment until you discover what the next move forward would be. Chad was not satisfied with partial fulfillment of his list. He decided to ask the woman on a date. While meeting a woman who checks off all the boxes is exciting, what was more exciting was how God was checking off all the boxes, showing Chad that He truly does hear our hearts and He cares about what matters to us. God cares about our relationships, and this would be a defining moment in Chad's relationship not only with the woman but also with God.

Well, you can fill in the rest of the story, and what came next was a happily married couple living for God and enjoying all that God has brought and continues to bring them both. My husband and I just celebrated our ten-year anniversary in 2020. We didn't get to celebrate the way we had planned due to COVID restrictions. We decided to stay close to home and simply enjoy each other's company. We thought about how our relationship was already in the making when Chad decided to make that list. There was one box on Chad's list that didn't get checked off until later in the relationship when he discovered that I also have a couple of tattoos. Just a cherry on top of the cake because God wanted Chad's list to be fully completed.

Now, I'm not saying that Chad's list is a model for building the perfect relationship or foundation for marriage. What I am saying is that sometimes God wants us to be dissatisfied, not discontent. Sometimes God wants us to be specific so that when He answers our prayers, we know without a shadow of a doubt that only He could have done this to completion. I was told that if I really wanted a successful marriage, I should hold off for a man who treats his parents well. While Chad was checking off boxes on his list, I was observing how he treated his family. We were both specific in our methods, and God answered both of us at the right time.

God has continued to show up for us in very specific ways over and over again, and we look forward to the day when we can share all of the ways God has built our marriage on a level the world is not familiar with, all for His glory.

PUZZLED TO PURPOSE
www.puzzled2purpose.com

"WHO ARE YOU WEARING?"

JASON & LUCINDA HART

Married ~ June 2005

"Therefore, as the elect of God, holy and beloved, put on tender mercies, kindness, humility, meekness, long-suffering; bearing with one another, and forgiving one another, if anyone has a complaint against another; even as Christ forgave you, so you also must do. But above all these things put on love, which is the bond of perfection." (Colossians 3:12-14, NKJV)

Every year at the Academy Awards, there is one must-watch tradition that many look forward to that has nothing to do with who wins what award for what movie. Before the show starts, the movie stars and celebrities parade themselves for the media and paparazzi on the red carpet. As they take pictures and make their grand entrances, the reporters and talk show personalities interview them and ask the most anticipated question of the evening: "Who are you wearing?" The answer to this question is the point of focus for every tuxedo or suit, every dress, even down to the shoes.

What seems to be most valued is what is on the outside; however, does that tell the whole story? This superficial concern for what the movie star is wearing becomes a story within itself that sucks in onlookers and clothing enthusiasts of all kinds. They look stunning outwardly, but often their lives of mishap and dysfunctional failing relationships are later brought to the light.

What is interesting is that many couples tend to operate the same way, emphasizing what is happening on the outside. It seems that the concern in a marriage (which we believe is perpetuated by the advent of this social media craze) is more about what the couple has accomplished, what possessions they have, how many vacation pictures they post online, etc. This puts pressure on others who follow them to add more to their plate in order to stay current with the culture. Today's world continually perpetuates the fallacy that what looks good is good, but we know that, truthfully, nothing powerful is built from the outside in.

What is most important is how couples are developing from the inside out. The Apostle Paul makes this clear when he says, *"Therefore, as the elect of God, holy and beloved…"* What he is saying is that you already have intrinsic value because God says you are valuable. First, you are *the elect of God*, which means you have been specifically chosen by God to be His own. Second, you are *holy*, which means two things: you are separated from the world and no longer part of it, and you live a different lifestyle that is contrary to the culture. Third, you are *beloved*. This means that God has a special affection towards you because you are valuable in His eyes.

Since you already have intrinsic value as a person who is chosen, holy, and beloved by God, there is a different set of values that you should operate in towards your spouse. Apostle Paul tells the saints to "put on" these values. What he is literally saying is that you are called to wear Christ at all times. No longer should you wear and display the values of the world.

What hurting marriages desperately need is a healthy value system that honors that sanctity of their marriage and guides them in how to create a workable and fulfilling relationship with one another. A value system is an inward disposition that is expressed outwardly in order to create cohesion and relatability with one another.

When you put on the values laid out by Apostle Paul, how powerful would your marriage be? How would you powerful would you show up daily? A marriage that puts on tender mercies, kindness, humility, meekness, longsuffering, bearing with one another, and forgiveness creates a culture of workability because it is highly valued. The last value that you are to put on is love. When you wear love, you wear God because God is love. Love is the bond of perfection, not because it makes one without mistakes, but because it is what connects the hearts of mature couples.

Dr. Henry Cloud once said, "On both the positive and the negative side, ultimately what you value is what you will have. If you value something in a relationship, you will not tolerate anything that destroys this value, and you will also seek to make sure it is present and growing. And because of these values, the relationship takes on an identity and form, a character of its own." You are what you value.

So now we ask you, "Who are you wearing?"

Live Hartstrong Marriage Coaching
www.wearehartstrong.com

R·E·S·P·E·C·T·

Respect your spouse for their strengths and never look down on them for their weaknesses.

Exhort your spouse daily. Everybody has flaws, and it's easy for us to point them out, and sometimes hold grudges. But if you as a couple respect your strengths in each other, it will build you and your spouse up and not tear you down.

Support each other in your dreams and endeavors.

Pray for one another always.

Celebrate each other, and all the good things that you see.

Trust the God in each other. By trusting the God in each other, you both should set out to respect your walk with God, and then you will continue to value and respect each other always.

Romans 12:10 (ESV)

"Love one another with brotherly affection. Outdo one another in showing honor."

Excerpt from SIMPLE SECRETS
Golden Nuggets from God's Word To Enhance your Marriage

SPIRITUAL INTIMACY

WES & NEESHA STRINGFELLOW

Spiritual Intimacy

What does spiritual intimacy have to do with my intimacy with my spouse? Everything. Believe it or not, it is important to seek the Lord about everything. God looks inside our hearts and wants us to yield every member, getting to know Him in a way where we feel safe and intimate with Him as well. In our quest for this closeness with Himim, we have to focus on:

1. **Devotion to God:** creating a sacred place to meet with the Lord and focus completely on Him, hearing His voice only.

2. **Fellowship with God:** talking to and communing with Him, causing us to become less distracted. The more we spend time with Him, the more we desire to spend time with Him.

3. **The Presence of God:** spending time basking in the presence of the heavenly Father through worship and prayer. When you know what that feels like, you never want to leave.

You don't want to wake up one day and find that you never really surrendered to the will of God. Many couples don't want to make the commitment together to say yes to God, let alone say yes to each other; however, this time of intimacy with God really can serve to sharpen us as individual couples. So often, couples really feel it's impossible to see change. They feel as if there is no hope. When this hopelessness comes, closing off your heart to your spouse is what you think is happening; in actuality, you are closing off your heart to God, and your relationship is destroyed with both God and your spouse. Shutting down is not the solution; it's just another barrier you put up, and it won't give you the true intimacy for which you long.

Begin by praying and asking the Lord to forgive you for shutting down, and then ask for your heart to be open to experience the true meaning of intimacy: intimacy formed by the Creator that can never be shattered or shaken, intimacy that leaves you wanting to come back for more.

Dear heavenly Father,

Thank You for allowing me to know that the most important intimacy I have is with You. This will allow me to know that I can lean and depend on Your love in every area of my life. Open my heart, Lord, to receive Your love and to learn how to remain in a place of intimacy with You, always.

In Jesus' Name, Amen

Conflict Resolution

The concept of choosing your battles is something we had to learn early on in our marriage. We laugh about this (and still get upset at times), but for almost 26 years, I have been tripping over Wesley's shoes. Now, let me explain. I have asked Wes countless times to please put his shoes out of harm's way, which, to me, would be in the closet. It does not matter where he takes them off; somehow, I always trip, fall, or stub my toe on shoes that he has left in the middle of the floor. I will reiterate, this has been happening for almost 26 years! This brings me to share that many times, we fight about the same things over and over again. I get frustrated, he gets frustrated, but there just do not seem to be any changes. What can bring about the change? I'm not sure! Of course, intentionality and wanting to change would seem logical, but guess what: nope! Not even having the best intentions will change a pattern that does not seem like a big deal to your spouse.

That's when we learned to choose our battles: fight every day about shoes in the middle of the floor, or look down, pick them up, and put them in the appropriate place? Yes, I'd rather have peace any day than fight over shoes. I choose sanity. Does it mean that I never fuss? No. It doesn't even mean that I smile and say, "That's okay, Wes; no problem, honey." It just means that I make a choice to see what traps are being set for me daily to upset our marriage. One of the reminders of why choosing our battles is so critical in our relationship is that we witness so many people who choose to live in an unhappy, ugly state over trivial issues.

Take inventory of all of the things that you have allowed to ruin your day when you could have just let them go, or revisited them at another time in a nonthreatening environment. Wes and I are still practicing this exercise, but it works, and eventually, what seemed so huge ends up not even bothering us. We all have pet peeves; what's yours? Let your spouse off the hook. They want to change, and I believe, in time, they will. I still get on Wesley's nerves about my driving techniques, but he has also learned to choose his battles.

It works!

*   *   *

In order to resolve conflict, the first question that should be asked is, "Why?" Why are we even having this argument in the first place? Since all conflicts have a root, what is the root of this conflict? And how do we figure it out so that we can take care of it?

In marital relationships, the most common root of conflict is "offense," and the most insignificant disagreements can turn ugly when "offense" rears its terrible head. Unless it is dealt with, when one partner gets offended, the fireworks begin to fly, the insults start rolling out, and one partner will walk away hurt. Sometimes we get offended by our spouse, and they are not even aware that they are being offensive!

Take the time to write down some of the things that hurt or offend you. Writing those things down can help you dig to the root of the matter. The offense could actually stem from some past hurt from a previous relationship, or even from something that happened to you in your childhood. The reality is that harboring pain and resentment of any kind is painful not only to you, but also to those around you.

Ideally, we should come into a marriage as whole and as healthy as possible. And even when there are problems, we should discuss our history with each other before the wedding. Our self-examination and wise counsel before *and* during the marriage can relieve hidden offenses and ultimately save the marriage.

1. **Choose to Forgive.** Yes, you have read correctly. Choose to Forgive is listed twice. Understand that forgiveness is quite possibly the most difficult part of any relationship and perhaps the greatest hurdle we will face in our marriages. It is not enough for couples to agree to forgive but never to forget. It is human nature for us to remember something that was painful, but God's Word commands us to forgive if we want our heavenly Father to forgive us.

2. **Forgive Without Punishment.** Unforgiveness will drain both partners of all of the vital nutrients that they need to be healthy in a relationship. But once forgiveness has taken place, one partner cannot continue to remind the other of his or her wrongdoing. We should never punish our spouses or withhold love from them. They are our partner and not our enemy. Once we have forgiven, it's over! The Word reminds us:

   "And when you stand praying, if you hold anything against anyone, forgive them, so that your Father in Heaven may forgive you your sins." (Mark 11:25, NIV)

"Make allowance for each other's faults, and forgive anyone who offends you. Remember, the Lord forgave you, so you must forgive others." (Colossians 3:13, NLT)

"For if ye forgive men their trespasses, your heavenly Father will also forgive you." (Matthew 6:14, KJV)

God has a great plan for all of us. Our marital conflict does not have to keep us from that plan. Remember, unforgiveness and offense are like a cancer that consumes us and spreads to those around us, but the cancer does not have to win! We already have the victory and the power to "rumble" productively and in love; that love is where our true power comes from. Consider these additional scriptures when planning your next "energetic discussion":

Willingness in Marriage

As the years go by, couples will face challenges. During the strenuous times of testing, we must continue to press in, even when it is uncomfortable. We must keep before us the repairs that must be done and receive the healing the Holy Spirit wants to bring to us. Most importantly, we have to resist the urge to point the finger at others, reminding ourselves of the Words of Jesus found in Matthew 7:3-11 (MSG):

"Don't pick on people, jump on their failures, criticize their faults—unless, of course, you want the same treatment. That critical spirit has a way of boomeranging. It's easy to see a smudge on your neighbor's face and be oblivious to the ugly sneer on your own. Do you have the nerve to say, 'Let me wash your face for you,' when your own face is distorted by contempt? It's this whole traveling

road-show mentality all over again, playing a holier-than-thou part instead of just living your part. Wipe that ugly sneer off your own face, and you might be fit to offer a washcloth to your neighbor."

"Don't be flip with the sacred. Banter and silliness give no honor to God. Don't reduce holy mysteries to slogans. In trying to be relevant, you're only being cute and inviting sacrilege.

"Don't bargain with God. Be direct. Ask for what you need. This isn't a cat-and-mouse, hide-and-seek game we're in. If your child asks for bread, do you trick him with sawdust? If he asks for fish, do you scare him with a live snake on his plate? As bad as you are, you wouldn't think of such a thing. You're at least decent to your own children. So don't you think the God who conceived you in love will be even better?"

The fight is worth it! We don't always understand that the past is affecting our present actions, yet when the knowledge of an issue has surfaced, it can positively change the entire pattern of our behavior emotionally, physically, spiritually, mentally, and sexually.

Couples should care for the well-being of each other's spiritual lives; however, the best thing you could ever do for one another is to pray and be patient while waiting on God to move. While you are praying and waiting, there are some things you can do:

1. Intentionally find couples who are healthy and begin to connect with them

2. Fill your time with purpose

3. Begin to journal or start a list of what you intend to let go of and what you intend to embrace

4. Above all, speak the Word, eat the Word, pray the Word (see Matthew 6:33)

If your spouse is open to it, pray together daily. If your spouse isn't very spiritually motivated, then try to keep prayer short. Concentrate on the quality of the prayer and not the length of the prayer. Don't force your spouse to pray; you can pray until he or she is comfortable enough to pray aloud.

THE BLAME GAME

Roy & Kimberly Manley

Married ~ June 1992

"And they heard the sound of the Lord God walking in the garden in the cool [afternoon breeze] of the day, so the man and his wife hid and kept themselves hidden from the presence of the Lord God among the trees of the garden. But the Lord God called to Adam, and said to him, 'Where are you?'

He said, 'I heard the sound of You [walking] in the garden, and I was afraid because I was naked; so I hid myself.' God said, 'Who told you that you were naked? Have you eaten [fruit] from the tree of which I commanded you not to eat?' And the man said, 'The woman whom You gave to be with me—she gave me [fruit] from the tree, and I ate it.' Then the Lord God said to the woman, 'What is this that you have done?' And the woman said, 'The serpent beguiled and deceived me, and I ate [from the forbidden tree].'" (Genesis 3:8-13 AMP)

Oftentimes in relationships we play what we call "The Blame Game." When you think of a game, there are always winners and losers. The focus of the Blame Game is a winner/loser perspective that creates a sense of competition within the relationship. Playing this type of game can get out of control and create things in the relationship that are hard to overcome.

The word "blame" means to assign a fault or a wrong to another, to accuse someone of what was done to you or for how you have acted in a given situation. It is the act of removing the responsibility from oneself and placing it onto another. When we blame, we attempt to shift the responsibility of a wrong we have committed onto our spouse to escape the results the wrong may present. In other words, you are making your spouse responsible for your behavior. No one is responsible for your behavior but YOU! When you don't have the right mindset and proper thought process towards your spouse, you will blame your spouse for everything. This mindset promotes the idea that "I'm not going to deal with me, I'm not going to deal with the inner me," and when you don't deal with the inner you, you make your spouse the "enemy." We blame others to avoid the guilt of what has happened in the relationship. This is an indication that we are unwilling to deal with the defense mechanisms we use in marriage against our spouse.

There are three reasons why we blame: 1) to protect ourselves 2) to avoid rejection, and 3) to minimize exposure of our insecurities. We shift the blame to keep the spotlight off of ourselves and to avoid uncovering and facing our insecurities. We avoid being honest and blame our spouse for our shortcomings. What you don't deal with, will eventually deal with you.

In Genesis chapter 3, Adam and Eve were faced with tossing the blame. God confronted Adam regarding the sin they had committed. God had told Adam not to eat of the tree of the knowledge of good and evil, and that to do so would result in death—a spiritual death, not a physical death.

These are the ways they tossed the blame:

1. **Avoiding the issue:** In verse 9, God asks Adam, "Where are you?" He avoids the question and responds, "I heard the sound of you walking." When you avoid the issue, you look for ways to minimize the real problem.

2. **Shifting the wrong:** In verse 11, God asks Adam, "Who told you that you were naked?" Adam responds to God by saying, "The woman you gave me..." and blaming Eve for giving him the fruit to eat. Remember, God did not ask him that. Adam shifts the wrong to make it all about the woman instead of what he did.

3. **Blinded to the wrong:** In verse 12, Adam says, "The woman you gave me, she gave me the fruit from the tree, and I ate." He was unwilling to face the decision he made. Often in the blame game, we turn a blind eye to what we've done and can only see what our spouse is doing. Before you can point the finger at them, remember, a finger is pointing back at you.

4. **Lack of responsibility:** In verse 13, God says to the woman, "What have you done?" Eve says, "The serpent deceived me." Notice that Eve now shifts the blame to the serpent. When you start to blame, it's never you! While Eve was not present in the natural when God gave Adam the instructions, she was, however, present spiritually, which meant she was responsible for the command that God gave. You may say, "How? She wasn't there." The scripture tells us that God caused a deep sleep to fall upon Adam, and he took one of Adam's ribs, closed up his flesh, and formed and shaped woman. She was a part of Adam; she was one with him, so she was there when God spoke to Adam. When the serpent spoke to Eve concerning which tree to eat, Eve said, "We are not to eat from the tree of the knowledge of good and evil." How could she say that? Did Adam tell her that? No. It's because she was there. She was just as responsible as Adam for the sin they had just committed.

So, before you shift the blame, take a moment to 1) make sure your reason is justifiable, 2) be honest with yourself, and 3) count up the cost—what will be the ultimate outcome.

Live Out the Vows Couples Ministry
www.theelitewife.com
kimberlycmanley@gmail.com

DISAGREE, BUT DON'T DISINTEGRATE

OLIVER & DENISE MARCELLE

Married ~ September 2000

We want to share something with you—something that may alarm you, or burst your bubble, so to speak. As long as you remain married, and as long as you are two different individuals, you're going to have disagreements. You are. It's just going to happen. You're going to go through some periods of time where you just don't see eye to eye on some things. However, we challenge you not to allow your disagreements to disintegrate your relationship.

We'll say it again for the people in the back: do not allow your disagreements to disintegrate your relationship.

There are many ways to accomplish this goal, but we're going to give you three that you can implement immediately:

1. **Remember that although you are striving for oneness, you don't always have to be the same. Oneness does not mean *sameness*.**

   We're all created differently.

   We've been married for over 20 years. Being together for that long does have its advantages. Sometimes we do know what the other one is thinking, and we use that to quickly course-correct and get on the same page. But because we're created differently, we're not always going to think the same thing. If we did, then one of us would not need to be here. Wow! Let that sink in for a minute…

   Because we're created differently, we're going to think differently. And that's okay. We don't get caught up in needing to think alike, and we don't get bent out of shape when we disagree (we've grown… it was not always like that). We aim to find the middle ground, to negotiate, to craft a game plan that's going to be the best thing for the relationship. It's not about either one of us individually, it's about the team and what's going to benefit the team. So remember, you don't have to think the same. The goal is oneness, not sameness.

2. **Be mindful of proximity. Use it to your advantage.**

   It's very difficult to have a "knock down, drag out" argument while you're close to each other. So, we encourage couples to be in close proximity with each other when having a disagreement or a difficult conversation. Don't try to have these disagreements and conversations over the phone, via text, or shouting at each other from across the room—or even from a different room. Make sure that you are sitting close to each other. When communicating from a distance, many things can be lost in translation. You don't have the advantage of seeing cues (body language, etc.) that can alert you to the need for additional explanation and clarification. So, use proximity.

3. **Avoid opening up a can of worms.**

Huh?!? What do we mean by that?!?

You've heard the phrase "opening up a can of worms"— doing or saying something that will make a situation even more complicated or unpleasant than it already is. We are challenging you to refrain from doing that in a disagreement. Don't open up a can of worms with trigger words or phrases like *"every time you..."* or *"you never..."* or *"you always..."* Why? Because that's going to put your spouse on the defensive. Once that happens, they're not going to hear anything else that you have to say.

This is one of the quickest ways to make your argument or disagreement disintegrate your relationships. So, choose your words, making sure to stay away from those trigger words/phrases. Also, don't bring up past issues into the current conversations. Work on the issue at hand and don't use trigger words that will open up a can of worms.

The book of Proverbs is packed with wise counsel about the use of words. Take some time to peruse the chapters to find the gems that will allow your communication to thrive and keep your disagreements from disintegrating your relationship.

> *"A gentle answer deflects anger, but harsh words make tempers flare."* (Proverbs 15:1, NLT)

www.denoli.org
admin@denoli.org

Sweet Sleep

Never go to bed angry. Make it a point to always end the evening with peace, even if there is only a small point of contact.

You might have a disagreement, but always connect before you go to sleep – it's a simple antidote for recovery and making up.

Ephesians 4:26 (MSG)

"Go ahead and be angry. You do well to be angry – but don't use your anger as fuel for revenge. And don't stay angry. Don't go to bed angry. Don't give the Devil that kind of foothold in your life."

Excerpt from SIMPLE SECRETS
Golden Nuggets from God's Word To Enhance your Marriage

ENGAGED

JERRY & CHRIS McQUAY

Married ~ December 1972

Our one-and-only baby girl recently got engaged, and we're thrilled *for* her and *with* her.

Almost immediately after her engagement, we heard several friends were also getting engaged, so this topic was already on my mind when I (Jerry) came across a blog post from one of my *virtual mentors*, Pastor Larry Stockstill, who says: "Everyone knows that when you decide to marry, you get *engaged*. Everyone does NOT know, however, that it is also the secret to *staying* married."

When love is not engaged, it is passive.

Chris has often reminded me that *love* is a verb—an *action* word. It's just as accurate that when love is not engaged, it's *passive.*

We know in order to stay "engaged" in marriage you must stay plugged into a power source. Anything unplugged will eventually die.

When couples stop engaging spiritually, intimately, emotionally, and conversationally, *it's just a matter of time.*

Technology can be the enemy of engagement.

When cell phones first came out *(yes, I'm old enough to remember),* I thought it would be amazing to always be able to stay in touch with Chris no matter where she was through this miracle of technology.

Little did I know that couples would sit for hours near each other but be immersed in their private technological space instead of using these mobile phones to increase their connection. "Their texts are brief, hard to read emotionally, and sometimes hilariously autocorrected!" Pastor Larry is right: Turn the phone off, look into each other's eyes, and ENGAGE.

Engagement is growing higher together.

I've noticed that I get bored when Chris and I are disengaged. Television can replace conversation. Even special events feel flat and unrewarding.

But when I engage Chris in a conversation, she pushes the subject higher, makes it more interesting, or often helps me see from a different perspective.

Engagement precedes discovery.

Couples disengage when they think they know everything there is to know about their spouse. Chris and I are almost 49 years into this marriage, and I realize that I've only scratched the surface of knowing this woman!

In the process, I'm learning that discovery is MY job. I must be such a good listener that I pick up on small statements that lead to whole new worlds of opportunity that we can explore together.

Engagement is taking full responsibility for everything.

I'm embarrassed to admit that there was no division of responsibilities in our home for the first half of our marriage. My mom had chosen to "spoil" me as the baby of our family, so I never learned to do anything around the house—no cooking, no laundry, no chores. Consequentially, I didn't lift a finger around the house after Chris and I married, and she picked up where my mom left off.

I honestly don't recall how God opened my eyes, but I'm thankful for the day I understood that being a leader means being responsible. Today there is nothing in our marriage that is "out of bounds" for me to do. The answer is "YES!" I don't ever again want to force Chris to silently carry an entire area of drudgery and duty by my passivity. I want to jump in there with her, get my hands busy, and *ENGAGE*.

Guys, don't you know that a "couch potato" partner is a *turn-off*? When you sit idly by while your spouse completes project after project, don't be surprised when you want to jump into bed and "engage" in sex!

I agree with Pastor Larry's conclusion: "You got engaged? Then GET ENGAGED. Plug in. Get off the phone. Stay 'with it.' It's true love."

CHRISTIAN LIFE CENTER
www.clc.tv

LOVE STORY

CHARLES & MERI HORTON

Married ~ June 1992

"Let us therefore make every effort to do what leads to peace and to mutual edification." (Romans 14:19, NIV)

Charles and I met in 1991 at a mutual friend's house party. Charles lived in LeClair Courts on the Southwest Side of Chicago, and I lived in Humboldt Park on the Northwest Side. Charles was raised in a two-parent African American household of thirteen, while I grew up in a Southern Baptist, Spanish-speaking Puerto Rican family of five.

I think it was our cultural differences that attracted us to each other initially. I was also very attracted to his bronzy toffee-and-copper undertones and lost myself in his luscious, full lips, not to mention the brightness of his flirtatious smile. I jokingly say that I married him to bring height to the family. I was very interested in Charles's background, and his perception of life and society. I was also really interested in African American culture. That sparked a lot of conversations between us, and we became excellent friends.

After some persistence on my part, we became a couple and fell in love. When we announced the news to our families, there were some initial concerns. "Being in an interracial marriage did open my eyes to things that I would never have thought about," Charles says. Some of his biracial friends had much worse experiences, having their hair cut off or being beaten up. Some had grandparents or other family members who disowned them. Between us, "race is not an issue," Charles says. "We forget about it until the outside world reminds us from time to time." "I'm blessed with having terrific friends who are receptive to our relationship," he says. "I don't think they think about the racial aspect of it unless something happens."

My family was opposed at first. It is not that they are... racist. They were just looking out for their daughter and her future, to the best of their ability. They believed blacks are more likely than whites to suffer medical conditions that lead to more severe health problems and higher health care and insurance costs as they grow older. These health problems are exacerbated by financial troubles that include lower savings and lower rates of homeownership. My parents did not want me to be part of that; they wanted life easier for me.

Charles's family also had a similar reaction. When he told his family that we were getting married, they questioned why he was marrying a Puerto Rican. He encouraged them to get to know me before they judged me.

What is clear to us is that being of a different race or ethnicity ultimately makes very little difference in a happy relationship. Instead, a couple's different cultures and background only seem to enhance their lives together.

When I told Charles stories of Puerto Rico, about the history, the music, the land itself, how my relatives lived in Puerto Rico, and all the amazing experiences and adventures they've had, Charles just wanted to grab his shoes, run to Puerto Rico, and be a part of it.

Equally, it's an absolute joy to be exposed to Charles's way of life. He took me to soul food restaurants and witnessed all the things he loves about his cultural background with a fresh pair of eyes.

Charles believes we need to be reminded regularly of the problems we still face as a society so that we can address them. Hopefully, seeing the struggles people have faced in the pursuit of love over something so trivial and irrelevant as skin color will change people's perspective—the ideal outcome being that we would get to a stage in society where the idea of interracial marriage is not an issue, but an accepted and normal part of society. Until this happens, films and other messages like this will always be important in making this a reality.

As a child, I loved seeing relationships such as Lucy and Ricky Ricardo from *I Love Lucy*. It reminds the world that Charles and I are not together because of our ethnicity—we are in love!

There need to be more and more stories told through the eyes of people who face prejudice and discrimination every day because without witnessing it properly, it is so easy to forget that it is there. "Plus, the more love stories told about relationships such as ours, the more people realize that we are just humans looking for our soulmates."

After a period, Charles and I found that our families learned to embrace and celebrate their cultural differences. We were married in 1992 and enjoyed a Christian ceremony.

We now live in Matteson, Illinois, a south suburban area of Chicago, and we have three children and two grandchildren.

MISSION POSSIBLE INSTITUTE
www.missionpossibleinstitute.com

HOW TO GET PAST YOUR PAST

H A S A N I   &   D A N I E L L E   P E T T I F O R D

Married ~ October 2002

Being joined together in marriage requires forgiveness, patience, and grace because no person is perfect, which ultimately means no marriage is perfect. We have all been recipient and contributor of emotional hurts and pains in marriage. None of us can make it in a marriage without experiencing some kind of pain.

The question is not "What do you do IF you experience hurt in your marriage?" The question is, "What do you do WHEN you experience hurt in your marriage?" Whether the incident happened a few weeks, a few months, or even a few years ago, the ultimate question is, "How do you heal the hurt in your marriage when you are haunted by the ghosts of your past?"

We are all familiar with the biblical story of Lot and his wife. God placed judgment on Sodom and sent an angel to deliver a message to Lot: "

Unfortunately, Lot's wife disobeyed God and looked back on her past life, and she was turned into a pillar of salt. This clearly demonstrates that there is something destructive about becoming stuck looking at our past.

Several years ago, I coached a woman who had experienced something traumatic that continued to plague her relationships with family, friends, and co-workers. While at a retreat, I took her through an exercise that demonstrated the damage of dwelling on her past. I instructed her to stand at one end of a room and face the opposite end, which was approximately thirty feet away. Though the room housed several pieces of furniture, there was a path that led from one end of the room to the other.

I told her to imagine that the wall opposite her represented her future and the wall behind her represented her past. I then instructed her to walk toward her "future" wall. However, before she took her first step, I asked her to turn around to face her "past" wall and walk backwards toward her future. As she took a few steps back, she bumped into a couch, then a chair, and then she stumbled over a coffee table. She quit her journey before making it to the other side of the room.

Immediately, she understood why she had spent the last three years living in pain. She realized that she had been looking at her future through the lenses of her past. Unfortunately, many of us who have experienced hurt in our marriage tend to live in the past and resist living in a new future. If our partner has lied to us, betrayed us, or disappointed us, we are not quick to forget. Instead, we build walls with bricks made of anger, resentment, hostility, vindication, and un-forgiveness.

We often relive a past event over and over and over again, perhaps thousands of times, simply by thinking about it. Sometimes we're conscious of our thoughts, and sometimes we're not. Every time we replay that painful experience in our minds, we train our bodies to remember and experience the suffering all over again. After a while, we don't even have to think about the past event to create that feeling. We've got it memorized. We've created our own suffering, and it's no longer our spouse hurting us. Instead, we are hurting ourselves by focusing on what our spouse has previously done, making it increasingly hard to have any hope for the future. As we begin to think about the future, we obsess over a worst-case scenario based on memories of our past, convincing ourselves that our spouse will never change.

Imagination begins to plan a future that reinforces the pain we are currently experiencing. The more we think about the possibility of our spouse cheating, lying, or hurting us, the more it negatively impacts our emotional state. Not only are we hurt by our past, we become frustrated and discouraged about our future, and we convince ourselves of the probability of a negative outcome. This is damaging because we are programming our bodies to experience a painful event that hasn't yet happened. Then, rather than taking the time to embrace our present reality, we jump back and forth from a painful past to an anticipated painful future.

The only way to break this cycle and change our reality is to change the way we think, feel, and act. Romans 12:1 (NIV) says, *"Do not conform to the pattern of this world, but be transformed by the renewing of your mind..."* In other words, we must think differently. If we renew our minds with a new way of thinking, we will break the patterns that have trapped us in our own pain. Because our minds are both records of the past and roadmaps to the future, we must leave our past in the past and anticipate a better future. When we have negative, fearful, or impatient thoughts, we begin to feel negative, fearful, and impatient. Likewise, when we have great, loving, and joyous thoughts, we produce chemicals that make us feel great, loving, and joyful.

We should use our bodies as tools that serve us. Instead of obsessing about some painful event that we fear is waiting for us, we must obsess about something good. Obsess about a new, desirable experience that we can wrap our emotions around. See and experience the marriage you want, not the one you have. See your spouse doing the right thing, not all the wrong previously done. See a better version of yourself, not the same person you've always been. Live in a new future, and as you begin to believe that you're experiencing the elevated emotions of a new future outcome in the present moment, you transform. You become more hopeful, optimistic, and willing to work on the restoration of your marriage.

COUPLES ACADEMY
www.couplesacademy.org

OUR 4-B PRINCIPLE FOR LIFE & MARRIAGE

TONY & RUBY POWELL

Married ~ May 2003

"Stop imitating the ideals and opinions of the culture around you, but be inwardly transformed by the Holy Spirit through a total reformation of how you think. This will empower you to discern God's will as you live a beautiful life, satisfying and perfect in his eyes." (Romans 12:2, TPT)

Marriage is hard... it takes work... it takes each of us working together. One of the main things that we learned a few years into our marriage is that we are a team, and that we will never win if we are playing on different sides. We are different in our ways of thinking and operating—Tony is the artist, Ruby is the analyst! Tony is flexible, Ruby is structured! Tony sings "Que Sera Sera," Ruby asks "What's the plan?" This could create quite the conflict if not managed properly. So, we developed a system that we call the 4-B Principle for our life and marriage. It is what some would call an oxymoron in that it is spiritual and yet practical. Over our years of marriage, Tony has become more structured and Ruby has become more flexible. We have committed to putting this into practice every day, and since its inception, we can count the times we've had anything more than an "energetic vocal disagreement." Let's take a look at these principles.

Number 1: Be Prayerful

We have found that we can get so much more done when we take the time to pray together. Not just praying for each other, and not just praying about each other, but praying together. We set time every morning to read a devotional and pray together. We take pleasure in coming together to commune with God. Our communion time with God helps maintain a high level of intimacy in our relationship. It does each of our hearts so much good to actually hear how we pray for one another's needs, desires, and concerns. It brings us joy to celebrate each other's victories when prayers are answered for us and for others. Through our prayer time, we realized how much we enjoyed spending time together.

Number 2: Be Patient

Patience is something that is needed in every area of marriage, and it doesn't just happen. It takes work to meld two very different adult personalities together. We had to learn that. If you know that God has put you together and that your marriage was truly made in heaven, don't fret! What God has put together let no one separate—not even you! We are not going to be able to get over the little things that drive each other crazy overnight; there are still some things that probably won't ever change, but we have learned that those differences have become our superpower together. Waiting patiently is not always easy, but the reward of patience is so much greater than the anxiety of whining and bellyaching.

Number 3: Be Proactive

Honestly, we think this is the best 'B' of the 4-B system! To be proactive is to get ahead of the game! We can't be reactionary! Being reactionary is not a good thing because anything that reacts often has volatile results. Don't wait until a situation gets to the boiling point. Love each other enough to deal with the hard questions when they first come up instead of waiting until they become a major problem and thus creating an oversized explosive. Remember that two different people with different upbringings, different personalities, different DNA, bringing different sets of luggage from the past (yes, we did say luggage and not baggage), etc., create very unique dynamics in the marriage. So, make a commitment to one another that you won't let molehills become immovable mountains... chop the molehill down before it grows.

Number 4: Be Permanent

If you said traditional vows, you probably said something like "until death do us part." This was not just something that sounded good in the moment. There is a lot that comes with this statement! It is preceded by "for better, for worse, for richer, for poorer, in sickness and in health, to love and to cherish"! This means for keeps! This is for life! This is forever! You have to be determined that you are staying together whether you like it or not! It is the time to dig in your heels and make a declaration that the deadly 'D' word will never be a reality in your marriage. Society has made divorce too easy. Apart from infidelity/adultery, the Bible does not support writs of divorce. Don't be afraid or ashamed to seek help when there are challenges that you two can't seem to figure out together. There are a multitude of Christian counselors who provide sound godly wisdom that will help your marriage remain permanent.

THE BLAME GAME ICU
www.theblamegame.us
tonyandruby@theblamegame.us

Fill Up The Love Tank

Practice actions that your spouse loves, not just what you love. Every couple's tank can run low at times, but do you know what fills up your spouse's love tank?

Ask your spouse often what they like . . . what they love. Then find ways to surprise them; it's a simple, powerful addition to your marriage.

Psalm 103:5 (NLT)

"He fills my life with good things. My youth is renewed like the eagle's!"

Excerpt from SIMPLE SECRETS
Golden Nuggets from God's Word To Enhance your Marriage

WHATEVER IT TAKES

CHRIS & NERISSA EDDEN

Married ~ October 1997

"Now I want you to realize that the head of every man is Christ, and the head of the woman is man, and the head of Christ is God." (1 Corinthians 11:3, NIV)

We have four boys. We have seen mountain tops, we have experienced valley lows, we have had many heartaches and heartbreaks. God gave us an opportunity to break away from the pain to allow our heartbeats to return, and now our hearts are devoted to a lifetime together. We want to encourage couples to do "whatever it takes" to restore your love. God has given us the gift of marriage; do whatever it takes to preserve your gift.

nerissaedden@gmail.com
cedden01@gmail.com

"DO SOMETHING ABOUT IT"

MYION & EBONY ROBERTS

Married ~ August 1999

Growing up, I'm sure most of you heard the statement "Well, if you don't like it, do something about it." The situation in which the statement was said would determine how you responded.

Being married now 22 years, we can honestly say that statement has challenged both of us in more ways than one. We have had to dig deep within ourselves to live out the covenant agreement of marriage in a way that truly honors God.

"Submit to one another out of reverence for Christ... each one of you also must love his wife as he loves himself, and the wife must respect her husband" (Ephesians 5:21, 33, NIV).

The road to this type of submission wasn't easy, but this journey has been worth the sacrifice.

You may have faced, or are still facing, some sort of wilderness experience that has left you feeling rejected, disrespected, undervalued, unsupported, unloved, and the list can surely go on. However, right in this very moment of reading the above statement, you may be thinking, "They are right, my spouse does make me feel _____," but did we say those feelings you are feeling were projected from your spouse? No!

And the even crazier part is that oftentimes we overlook, extend grace, and even accept those projected behaviors or feelings from everyone else except our spouse, making submitting to each other an almost impossible feat.

Why is that? We're glad you asked!

In our 22 years of "doing something about it," we have learned that open, honest communication is key. That for us, everything begins and ends with God directing it all. Believe me when I say we've been through some wilderness experiences from being homeless (twice), evicted, repos, fighting, and the list goes on, I am amazed at how we are still standing to tell the story.

It really is because of this scripture that we were able to come out of some things.

"And they overcame and conquered him because of the blood of the Lamb and because of the word of their testimony, for they did not love their life and renounce their faith even when faced with death" (Revelation 12:11 AMP).

In really reading that passage, it made me think, am I being the best wife I can be? Do I even know what being a wife truly looks like? Am I being honest with where I am, how I feel, and what I need? The answer for me was no, so how could I ask my husband to be all those things I needed when I didn't even know what they were myself? So I had to take it back to "overcoming by the blood of the Lamb." That very scripture gave me strength in a way that I knew that for any obstacle I have faced or will face, the blood has already been poured over it. I knew that my feelings were valid, but sinning because of them is not what pleased the Father. That once I truly believed in that blood that has kept me thus far, I could speak about how good God has been to me, to my husband, to our children for the benefit of our family. It then made it easier to speak about where we've been, how we overcame, and what God is doing in our lives now to help us be sustained in Him.

There is power in your story, in your struggle, in your coming out of the fire, in your testimony. When we begin to speak life, we live, and even after we leave this earth, our words still remain. What are you speaking?

It is important to remember the covenant we agreed to on our special day, and that even when faced with obstacles, challenges, or differences, we stand and fight, war, decree, pray, tear down, build up, and love. We believe that is exactly what the Father did and continues to do for us. For us, taking everything back to the

Word of God concerning every area of our lives is what gives us strength. The scriptures shared in this passage have been food in times we needed to "do something about" where we were at the time.

We hope you enjoyed our devotional insert and that it sparked something within you to know you are overcomers and to use your testimony to help others so that they overcome as well. We speak an abundance of favor, health, grace, long life, peace, and love over each of you. Amen!

meandkbooks@gmail.com

TWO SHALL BECOME ONE

M A R K & D A V A R O G E R S

Married ~ July 1992

What is marriage? I honestly had no clue. I didn't know or understand what it was to be a wife, let alone a Kingdom wife. Mark and I have been married almost 30 years with three beautiful adult children. What surprises people is when we share that the last four years have been the best years of our marriage. This is due to our embracing and walking in the belief of a Kingdom marriage, understanding the concept of both the three-cord strand and two becoming one.

We both had the renewed desire to change as we hungered and thirsted after those things that God wanted for us individually and for our marriage, sharing how these things made our marriage stronger. Our prayer is that those revelations to us will be a blessing to you and your marriage.

Kingdom Marriage

A Kingdom marriage is one in which both walk in the knowledge of the following verses:

> *"Submit to one another out of reverence for Christ."* (Ephesians 5:21, NIV)

> *"Though one may be overpowered, two can defend themselves. A cord of three strands is not quickly broken."* (Ecclesiastes 4:12, NIV)

> *"But I want you to realize that the head of every man is Christ, and the head of the woman is man, and the head of Christ is God."* (1 Corinthians 11:3, NIV)

Being out of the order that God wants for marriage leaves more room for Satan to come in and operate against you. We know he is a liar and will attack the vulnerable areas, making you believe in some cases that your spouse is the enemy. The point is, Satan will attempt to use any means to cause chaos, division, distractions, mistrust, and anything that attacks and comes against marriage and family (Ephesians 6:12).

However, when we are in line with the way God ordained marriage, we are protected under His mighty wings covering our marriages with love, wisdom, knowledge, and forgiveness. Once one understands that all the strands work together to form the covenant of marriage, the bond between God, the husband, and the wife is a Holy Alliance, and a Kingdom marriage is birthed. In embracing God's order of how marriage should be, our purpose is revealed. Just as we have individual purpose, I believe we have divine purpose in marriage when the husband is the head under Christ.

At least that is how it was for us. We both shifted our perspective on the points above when we realized that only with God being first in our individual lives could we truly be manifested from being two to being one. I'm not saying we didn't know this, but come on, we all know there is a big difference between knowing something and actually believing it, doing it, and walking it out. It's as if you are going from being in competition with someone to collaborating and embracing another part of your being.

One important thing we learned was that not all spiritual warfare is the enemy warring against us; it can also be us warring against God's perfect and divine will for our lives and marriages. If you have not already done so, I ask you to focus on God and see yourself for the Kingdom husband and Kingdom wife that you are.

Have you ever looked at your spouse as the son or daughter of God that they are? If not, please do, as it will change your perspective and actions. Once we began to see one another as God's child, the barriers of unforgiveness were shattered and the love that God wanted us to have appeared. Prayers became more effective. When you do this, divine doors and opportunities occur. God's agenda is downloaded to carry out His Kingdom work as a reflection of His love for you and your spouse in your marriage.

Reflection

What steps can you take this week to embrace what a three-cord strand means to you and how it relates to your marriage as well as you personally?

What action will you take now that you understand your role as a spouse in a Kingdom marriage?

Prayer

Heavenly Father, thank you for our marriage. I pray it will continue to be everything that the Word of God called it to be. You are the head of our home and at the center of all we do. As it says in Ephesians 5:25, a husband's love is to be as Christ's love is for the church. Instill in my husband/wife the mighty man/woman and father/mother you have called them to be. Increase our hunger to know You and to seek Your wisdom guiding our thoughts, words, and actions, Father. I break every limitation the enemy has placed upon our lives that has hindered us from reaching our full potential for Your Glory. I pray that You will breathe life into our marriage, our callings, and our purpose. May the foundation upon which Christian marriage and the family unit are established remain firmly rooted in You, Father.

Amen.

MARRIAGE CEOS: FROM THE BEDROOM TO THE BOARDROOM

D W I G H T & D E I D R A R O U S S A W

Married ~ August 1998

In a marriage, both spouses should be intentional about becoming teammates! In order to become effective teammates, an authentic friendship should be established, and that friendship should be unmovable and unshakable.

When a man and a woman make the solid, unwavering decision to come together and live together as husband and wife, one of the implications of their vows is that they will be there to support the growth of each other in everything that is good. So, when they become a couple, they begin to work together on all that they formerly used to do independently.

This was what God was saying in the book of Genesis when he blessed Adam and Eve. He told them both to "be fruitful and multiply":

> *"And God blessed them. And God said to them, 'Be fruitful and multiply and fill the earth and subdue it and have dominion over the fish of the sea and over the birds of the heavens and over every living thing that moves on the earth.'"* (Genesis 1:28, ESV)

Understand that this blessing did not end at bearing children but would involve all that they worked together on; this included being fruitful in their businesses as well. They were saddled with the responsibility of dominating everything and everywhere together.

So, the idea of having a working husband and wife is not out of the Bible's context. It happened in the days of old, and so it is today as well.

However, the husband and wife must allow the wisdom of God to lead them in how to balance both the business and marriage, and how to make things work well.

Here are eight steps you can take to guide you on this path:

1. **Work Together**

   We see a couple working together in the case of Priscilla and Aquila from Acts 18. They were a couple who had a business of tentmaking and were preachers of the gospel as well. They worked together and did everything on one accord.

If you want to balance your business and home, you must share the same mindset, not necessarily working in the same place or the same trade but understanding the demands of each other's occupations in order to make allowances for shortcomings at home.

2. Encourage Each Other

This is a point you don't want to underrate. When work is going awry for one partner, the other must be a pillar of support and take things up where things are lacking at home. When you observe a deficit in effort to invigorate the other spouse, talk to them and encourage them through whatever may be wrong, thereby being burden-bearers to each other. (Galatians 6:2). The sign of true oneness is that when people look, they cannot trace weakness to a spouse, but both are seen as one.

3. Pray Together

The power of the fervent, unceasing prayer of a righteous couple is effectual in its working (James 5:16). Learn to pray together about situations which are challenging in the business or at home. There is NO substitute for prayer.

4. Take a Break Together

Whether it is a date night out or a stay-at-home break together, it will do a lot of good to relieve stress and tension. This is a good time to listen to each other and build up love and understanding again.

5. Keep an Open Communication Line

Without effective communication, there is no hope for progress. The people of Babel had their communication gift taken from them, and look what happened. If you want to go far and do well in your walk together, then communication must never be lacking. Talk to each other on every matter and gain understanding (Amos 3:3).

6. **Depend on Each Other**

Your spouse should be the first person you tell about anything that bothers you. Doing this will improve understanding and trust between you two. Don't go outside of the marriage looking for who can do this and that for you; seek your spouse for insight.

Depend on each other wholeheartedly, so that the business and the family life will naturally fuse into each other, and you will become true helpers to one other.

7. **Seek to Improve**

No person has attained the zenith of perfection in doing everything that is good, which means that we still have a lot of learning to do. There is still room to improve upon communication skills, patience, love, understanding, etc., as these are the elements you need for a balanced life of help and understanding that will pull you through the challenges that will storm against your business and home, and even the ones that will come from the struggle to balance both. Have an open mind of meekness; to be meek means to be flexible enough to learn without pride (Proverbs 16:16).

8. **Get Help When You Clearly Need It**

Again, no one knows it all, and sometimes you will be faced with almost impossible situations. When you have talked between yourselves and agree that you need some help from someone who is able to provide that help, then go for it. Don't keep on trying to make things work with the same formula that has proven not to work. It takes great effort to make things work seamlessly from business to home, so there's no need to feel shame asking for some help (Proverbs 19:20).

It is truly difficult to balance the demands at work and the demands at home, but these ideas should help any married business couple to rise above any limitations that should challenge them.

We've been in business since 1999 and ministry since 2009. It hasn't always been easy, but we were determined to have a balanced lifestyle as a married couple in the marketplace. Our couple's devotion was a key component! Praying and reading the Bible TWOgether was a game changer! Date nights and forgiveness allow you to continue to grow in grace and knowledge!

MARRIAGE CEOs
TWOGETHER MARRIAGES
info@twogethermarriages.org
www.twogethermarriages.org

THE 15-MINUTE COURTSHIP

JEEVA & SULOJANA SAM

Married ~ August 1983

*"I give you a new commandment—to love one another.
Just as I have loved you, you also are to love one another."*
(John 13:34, NET)

After a lengthy "courtship" that lasted all of 15 minutes, we decided to get married. Puzzled?

You see, ours was an arranged marriage in the Indian tradition, where matches are made by parents, often with the help of a marriage broker. Parents entrust this go-between with a "shopping list" of their preferences such as age bracket, education level, profession, income, faith, socio-economic background, looks, personality, and character. The broker then connects the parents of a man and a woman in his inventory who appear to be suitable matches for each other.

Our elders grudgingly allowed us to meet for 15 minutes by ourselves to have a conversation about the things that mattered to us (thanks to the hard bargain driven by our broker). Since many in India get married without ever meeting their future spouse in person ahead of time, it was viewed as a rather lengthy courtship! And then it was up to us to make the decision.

You are probably wondering how we could make such a life-changing decision in such a short time, without an extended dating or courtship period to get to know each other. Yes, we admit it is in stark contrast to Western culture, where the emphasis seems to be upon ensuring that you've found the right person before making the commitment of marriage. Co-habiting is often seen as a "trial marriage" to ensure that you can actually do life together.

In contrast, as children steeped in the Indian culture, we believe that since our parents know us better than anyone else, they are more equipped than we are to find our spouse for us. They do the "background checks" on our behalf through family and friendship networks. We trust, respect, and value their judgment. We avoid the hassle of chasing and catching our "perfect" partner after going through a number of "imperfect" ones, breaking hearts, and having our hearts broken in the process.

Please understand that we are not in any way putting down the process of dating or courtship. All three of our children found their spouses without an assist from Mom and Dad. Not that we did not offer to arrange their marriages, but the offer was politely declined by all three (sob, sob!).

Let's make one thing clear, though. Whether your parents arrange your marriage or you arrange it yourselves, ultimately, whether your marriage succeeds or not is entirely up to you. It is not just about finding the right person to marry, but also about being the right person for the one you marry.

We did not romance each other first. We chose to love each other first, and then romance followed. Can you wrap your head around that? That is normal in an arranged marriage. In other words, when we saw each other that day, we were not expecting to fall in love, we were hoping to make a choice to love. Love is always a choice. Isn't that what Jesus is saying in John 13:34?

So, what weighty matters did we talk about during our 15-minute courtship?

Jeeva: I wanted to make sure that Sulojana knew what life was going to be like in Canada. We would have no help from anyone else, no "maid service" as was often the norm for middle-class families in India. I also asked her if she knew how to cook. She lied and said "yes."

Sulojana: It wasn't exactly a lie. I knew how to boil an egg, and I was confident I could learn how to cook other dishes while waiting for my Canadian visa to be approved—a grace period of at least three months.

Jeeva: We got married ten days later and went on a short honeymoon. I returned to Canada the following week and began the immigration process for Sulojana. We were hoping it would only take three months, only to discover that Immigration Canada moves at the speed of sound, not light. It took nearly six months before her visa was approved.

Sulojana: That was not a total loss. My grace period to take cooking lessons was extended by three more months! I finally joined Jeeva in Canada in February 1984, recipe book in hand. You bet I knew how to cook!!

We are pleased to report that, as of August 18, 2021, the choice we made to love each other following a 15-minute courtship has turned into 38 years of marriage.

www.thesams.ca
jeevasam@gmail.com

Shhhh... Are You Listening

Take the time to listen with your whole heart. Listening with your whole heart means you hear me even without words. Nothing should catch you off guard if you are listening. Every spouse should be aware when changes are taking place.

Listen out for what your spouse is really saying – be attentive to the heart of the matter. If you are listening, you will avoid many pitfalls and traps along the way of life.

Stop talking so much – quiet your spirit and listen to what is being said from the heart.

Luke 6:45 (NASB)

"...for his mouth speaks from that which fills his heart."

Excerpt from SIMPLE SECRETS
Golden Nuggets from God's Word To Enhance your Marriage

SEXUAL EXPLORATION

J. GREGORY & CHEVELTA SMITH

Married ~ June 1992

We love to travel and explore different parts of the world. Each location we travel to creates a different experience, feeling, and awareness. Together, we have embarked on an intentional journey to discover new places, ideas, and revelations. Each experience takes us to new heights as we build deeper intimacy within our marriage. We simply follow the map to our desired destinations.

Did you think we were talking about traveling to Europe? The Bahamas? Or some faraway destination? Maybe we were! Or maybe we were talking about exploring the various erogenous zones on your spouse's body that would likewise create a different sexual experience, feeling, and awareness.

Much like normal travel, there are popular attractions and destinations that spouses often travel to immediately when exploring one another sexually. Although there is nothing wrong with commonly traveling to the same place, it can often inhibit one's ability to discover those exciting and hidden treasures of stimulation. Sexual exploration is a key element in discovering those exciting and hidden erogenous places (zones) on one another's body. "Erogenous" simply means those areas distributed throughout the body which are very sensitive to sexual stimulation. When these sensual locations are discovered, they will often lead to new ideas and revelations for couples to utilize in building exciting, healthy, and authentic sexual intimacy and love-making within their marriage.

So, how do you find these sensual areas? By mapping it out! Yes! Body mapping is a very exciting activity in which couples travel to various locations of each other's bodies using various types of touching to find those erogenous areas that lie hidden. The primary goal of body mapping is working together, as a couple, to explore and discover the most sensitive part of each other's bodies. As husbands and wives discover these various sensitive erogenous locations throughout each other's bodies, they should map out these specific spots mentally in their mind, in order to follow them to an ultimate destination of heightened climax and pleasure during future moments of intimacy.

Have you ever traveled behind the ear of your spouse? What about behind the thigh or above the gluteal cleft? Did you realize that the nape of the neck can be an erogenous zone for many? There are so many wonderful places to discover on your partner's body. Moreover, what's even more fun is discovering what type of touch creates sexual excitation in your partner (light vs. firm or gentle biting, sucking, licking, etc.). Remember, God not only created sex, but He intentionally placed these erotic sensations within our bodies for our sexual pleasure. As a result, we believe that it is our responsibility (as married couples) to make the time to intentionally embark on the journey of sexual exploration, with the primary goal of finding these erotic locations within the body of your mate. We encourage you to take the sexual exploration journey.

> *Dear Lord, we pray that you bless our marriage in the area of sexual intimacy. We pray that the sexual health of our marriage be whole, strong, and fulfilling. Give us complete freedom in exploring and "knowing" one another sexually. Let our desire be only for one another, without distraction. Let our sexual passion forever burn for one another all the days of our marriage union.*

www.drchevelta.com

"DO YOU SEE WHAT I SEE?"

H E N R Y & R O Z S T U T T L E Y

Married ~ June 2003

"Where there is no vision, the people perish...." (Proverbs 29:18, KJV)

We were ecstatic to receive a $12,000 bonus, our first bonus received from a place of employment during the early years of our marriage. Roz fell out of the chair when she learned about this bonus from her manager, and she came home and asked me, "Is this illegal?"

Six years prior, we were living from paycheck to paycheck. It was extremely tight financially. I was praying over each check we received into our home, "Father, please give us increase and direction on what you will have us to do with our finances. Let us be lenders and not borrowers." I consistently spoke life in our finances and spoke what I could not see in the natural.

And in fact, I remember one day I was on the phone with a customer service rep, and they asked if my and my wife's gross income combined was under $40,000 a year. I had to confess with an embarrassing feeling, "Yes, it is."

Yet every time we received compensation, we would faithfully tithe, sow offerings and first fruit. Our bills somehow got paid, and we experienced God's supernatural provision over and over.

As God continued to open doors in our careers through multiple promotions, graduate degrees, and certifications, we continued to pray about our finances and remained good stewards over what God entrusted to us by giving and sowing financial seeds.

I must be transparent, neither Roz nor I were taught how to manage money when were growing up. We both had credit card debt in college, we took out cash advances against credit cards while paying the minimum due, and we both had student loan debt connected with our undergraduate studies. But God dealt with the both of us individually and collectively.

As He weaved our lives together, and we began acknowledging Him in all our ways and asking Him to direct our paths, He taught us through His Spirit and the Word of God to be more disciplined with our resources, to pay off balances on credit cards when due, to live within our means, and to be content and not buy things we really couldn't afford.

Over the years, we have also set some goals for our marriage including getting Roz braces, purchasing a single-family home, becoming landlords, and paying off car notes and student loans.

God has allowed us to obtain these goals. To God be all the Glory! He has also been faithful to us through the pandemic, allowing us to continue striving toward financial freedom.

I am joyful! God has exceeded my imagination since those early days of praying over our paychecks. He has blessed us to achieve so much, and there's much more coming.

I declare wealth over my family!

And I decree and declare we shall be debt free in the name of Jesus!

Now, do you see what I see?

KEEP THE FIRE BURNING MARRIAGE
Ministry, Team Leaders
rosilynnlstuttley@hotmail.com

THE SECRET SAUCE
IN YOUR MARRIAGE

CHRIS & LAURA WHITE

Married ~ February 1996

I always dreamed of a happily-ever-after marriage, and I finally met my Prince Charming. My husband, Chris, intrigued me right away with the calmness that he brought to the relationship. I loved his logical, detail-oriented thinking. He had big dreams, goals, and a vision for his life. I came from a family of nine, and it was always chaos around us trying to get through each day. I knew I was destined for greatness, so I needed stability and direction, and Chris provided that for me.

We met at church and recognized quickly that God had brought us together. Nevertheless, in our earlier years of marriage, we started realizing there were some personality differences, and something was just not right in our relationship. We began having communication issues, and although it was nothing major, we knew that we were not on the same page.

Many times, we begin marriage with an idea of what marriage should be; however, as the years pass, we ask ourselves, "What is going on?" In most marriages, opposites attract—people are infatuated with those who are the opposite of who they are. We are intrigued by the variety of how the other person thinks, acts, and talks, as well as the diverse flavor they bring to the relationship.

However, these diversities can cause issues in life, especially when it comes to communication within your marriage. When you crack the communication code and learn how to communicate effectively, it will change the dynamics of your marriage.

We knew we were in our marriage for the long haul! Our belief is that what God has joined together, let no man separate. We would do anything to protect our marriage and make it better. Through much prayer and great books on marriage and communication, we discovered a few things that changed the course of our marriage. As you read on, our prayer is that these communication tips will provide insight and encouragement for your marriage, and they will make an impact in your marriage relationship.

The first thing we discovered is that we were speaking two different languages. My husband was serving me how he wanted to be loved, and I was serving him how I wanted to be loved. Gary Chapman's book *The Five Love Languages* was a game-changer for us. We took his quiz and discovered that my husband's love language was Acts of Service and mine was Affirmations. You may think that learning your love language is not a big deal, but it was life changing for us.

One thing that will get marriages into trouble is assuming rather than communicating with each other. The way you solve communication issues is to simply ask your partner what you want to know. Ask each other for specific details about your love language and what makes you feel loved. We made lists for each other, and the transformation in our communications and level of intimacy in our relationship flourished when we served each other in our respective love languages.

After we both completed the DISC assessment, which identifies your personality as well as your strengths and limitations, God gave me another revelation about our communication challenges. We realized how different we are in our thinking and communicating. My husband is one who thinks to speak, while I speak to think. In my coaching sessions when we begin discussing communication in relationships, the type of communicator is quickly identified. Whether in married couples or business-related relationships, this realization is an eye-opener to unresolved issues.

As I said, my husband is logical and detailed, so he thinks things over in his head, analyzes it, mulls it over, and when he is ready to share, he is pretty much done with the conversation. I, on the other hand, am just getting started. I want to know why, what, how, and what's next. When I asked questions and wanted to discuss things out loud, he used to think I was questioning, doubting, or not trusting him. There was tension in the air, and many times it led to arguments.

After we realized that we think and process things differently, we cracked the code to better communications in our marriage. Now, Chris does not get irritated or annoyed that I ask questions or when I want to talk out loud to process something.

The *secret sauce* to having a happy marriage is knowing your and your spouse's communication style as well as your love languages. If you give grace to each other as you learn to communicate the way you are wired and identify if you think to speak or speak to think, you can quit fighting the difference and embrace it, and it will make your marriage blossom.

> *"Be completely humble and gentle; be patient, bearing with one another in love. Make every effort to keep the unity of the Spirit through the bond of peace."* (Ephesians 4:2-3, NIV)

www.lifecoachlaurawhite.com

ALWAYS TALK TO ME

LEON & TRACY WRIGHT

Married ~ July 2020

"Do two people walk hand in hand if they aren't going to the same place?" (Amos 3:3, MSG)

Communication is a huge factor in any relationship, whether it be in a marriage, friendship, or kinship. In any relationship, you must communicate. Not communicating sends the wrong signals the wrong message. If Leon brought me flowers every day and put them in the kitchen, he would think that I like it and that they make our home look beautiful. If I don't communicate to Leon that I don't really care for live flowers, then how would he know? Or, if I don't say, "I would rather you get me something I can use or something I can keep," then he will continue to waste money on something that I would only look at for a few minutes and then go about my day. But if he buys me something I can use, he would see me use that gift for a really long time. For example, if it's a dress, that would become my go-to dress every time I go somewhere special.

So, you see why communication is so important. It saves time and money.

Just like with gifts, it is important to communicate what you like and don't like in a relationship: what makes you mad, what hurts your feelings, what makes you happy, what turns you on. Use your voice and say it. Be fair, give your spouse the cheat sheet to win your heart.

As men, we typically have a hard time relaying our true emotions and feelings because of the way we feel we will be perceived. A lot of us tend to walk around very guarded because we feel as if we have to protect our ego and our manhood. We do not like being or feeling vulnerable because we think it weakens us. For some strange reason, we are taught not to show our true emotions or talk about how we really feel. Your spouse should be the one person you can be vulnerable with, because your weaknesses should be covered by their strengths, and vice versa. If your spouse struggles in the area of communicating, or struggles with the vulnerability of sharing their feelings and thoughts, make sure you help them overcome it by providing them a safe space to open up to you.

When it comes to being in a relationship, communication is being able to share *and* understand each other's thoughts and feelings. It is important to always share your feelings, but it is equally important to understand your spouse's emotions and views. In order to effectively communicate, you have to be able to understand and respect each other's points of view. It is easy to just "get it off your chest," but it is a lot harder to understand where your spouse is coming from. Sharing *does not* mean yelling. Sharing *does not* mean getting the other one told. Sharing means expressing your thoughts and feelings in a tone that can be properly received by the other party. For instance, if you were to share a piece of your sandwich with another individual, you wouldn't throw the portion you want to share at them and expect them to still eat it and not be mad. No, you would take what you want them to have and present it to them in such a manner that they will gladly accept it and eat it. If the presentation is done poorly, then they won't want to eat your sandwich. In essence, you will have wasted a portion of your food for nothing. Communication and sharing your thoughts and feelings are the same way. You have to present it in such a manner that the other one will gladly accept it; otherwise, you will have just wasted valuable information.

When we fail to understand one another, our presentation of sharing is most likely going to be done poorly. I've discovered over time that many of our arguments and disagreements have been because we didn't really understand each other, when in actuality, we were saying the same thing, just from different aspects. You may not have a problem with sharing, but do you understand?

ONE DESTINY COUPLES MINISTRY
www.wearegreatness.org
wearegreatness@yahoo.com

LOVE IS A MIRROR

S TEVEN & L A V ONE Y ARBROUGH

Married ~ November 1999

"So husbands ought to love their own wives as their own bodies; he who loves his wife loves himself. For no one ever hated his own flesh, but nourishes and cherishes it, just as the Lord does the church." (Ephesians 5:28-29, NKJV)

People usually give the most attention to the things which they value and truly love at heart. Oftentimes, we go to great lengths in making sure our physical bodies, clothing, and cars are uniquely cleaned. We all have special preferences in soaps and cleaning processes for our laundry, dishes, and car washes.

During the COVID-19 pandemic, a strict protocol was placed on every household, individual, and business to wash hands at length and to sanitize everything imaginable.

The pandemic caused great problems with supply and demand in obtaining hand sanitizers, bleach, and disinfectants. These once basic household items could not be found anywhere, including local retail stores. On the other hand, now that the tide of the pandemic has come to a halt, local stores are now overstocked with disinfectants and hand sanitizer. These items can be located in most government buildings, personal homes, and local stores.

At the same time, the tide of struggling marriages seems to beat the shores of many households. There is a demand for marriages to be strengthened with the love the relationship truly deserves. The good news is, the love of Christ is available during times of peace or disaster. We are commanded by the Word of God to build up our spouses and encourage them. Husbands have been given the responsibility to give their wives a loving make-over the way that Christ Jesus washes and cleanses His people. Wives have been given the responsibility to submit to this unconditional, unfailing, loving make-over.

Husbands, when you love your wives just as Christ embraces His people, you shape and mold a wife who resembles yourself. Why not create a better you? The husband and wife are a reflection of each other; remember that love is a mirror.

The Word of God says:

"Husbands, love your wives, just as Christ also loved the church and gave Himself for her, that He might sanctify and cleanse her with the washing of water by the word, that He might present her to Himself a glorious church, not having spot or wrinkle or any such thing, but that she should be holy and without blemish." (Ephesians 5:25-27, NKJV)

YARBROUGH COACHING AND CONSULTING
yarbroughcoaching@gmail.com

Date Forever

It is so important to schedule a regular date night for a lifetime. Make this a priority – we can get bitten by the boring bug in our marriage if we don't.

Spice it up and be intentional about scheduling time to romance each other. Sometimes its good to schedule dates with other married friends. It does not replace your date night, but it is a bonus to connect with people who have the same values for their marriage.

> Proverbs 5:18-19 (ESV)
>
> "Let your fountain be blessed, and rejoice in the wife of your youth, a lovely deer, a graceful doe. Let her breast fill you at all times with delight; be intoxicated always in her love."

Excerpt from SIMPLE SECRETS
Golden Nuggets from God's Word To Enhance your Marriage

GODLY COMMUNICATION: CAN YOU JUST HEAR ME OR ARE YOU LISTENING?

MARC & RHONDA WHITE

Married ~ May 1998

One of our first arguments occurred a few months after we got married, and it centered around the temperature in our house. Marc was raised in a home where the air conditioning was rarely on in the summer. I, on the other hand, lived with my mom again right before I got married, and she insisted that after living with my father who rarely turned the air on, she would never be hot again in her life! As a result, we sat in our house with blankets over us in the summer.

Now, both scenarios may seem extreme, but in fact, Marc and I had each determined that our own way was correct. And the change in temperature was a definite trigger for both of us. We definitely had not learned to communicate what our experiences had been and how they were impacting our feelings or actions. Instead, we yelled (or I did), and we both said some things that were not so nice. I ended up trying to sleep in the basement where it was a bit cooler, and Marc stayed upstairs sweating.

Needless to say, years later, we've landed on what is best for us regarding this matter, which encompasses a little of both of our previous lives. Coming to an agreement through conversation was when the temperature in our home finally began to cool down. It might have been the first time that we listened for understanding instead of listening to respond. Godly communication that includes this type of listening is the only way we can ever consider having a marriage that lasts beyond our "baby love" season and grows into something that is everlasting.

We spend so much of our lives on trying to be heard. As infants, we cry loud enough to get fed; then, as toddlers, we whine loud enough to get our way. As teenagers, we huff enough to get grounded, and as adults, we spend our time making our points and trying to win in every way to feel justified. Even if you aren't a verbally assertive person by nature, your silence in situations speaks volumes. But what is the difference between being heard and being listened to? Does one have more value than the other? Does it make a difference?

It's been said that hearing is through the ears, but listening is through the mind. Most of the time in marriage, we hear what our spouse says with our ears, but we are formulating our response with our minds. That is why a majority of our conversations are less effective than they could be. Hearing is physiological, while listening is psychological. A person may be able to hear specific sounds but not be able to interpret the meaning. How many times in your marriage have you said something, only to have it interpreted in a completely different way than you intended? It may not be what you said but how your spouse heard it that makes the difference. Effective listening requires an effective listener. Such a person is patient and genuinely wants to understand for the betterment of the relationship. To listen and understand validates the speaker and confirms your love for them. Essentially, the effective listener has a bigger responsibility than the speaker, yet in marriage we often place more blame on what is being said instead of what has been comprehended.

Godly communication in marriage involves some simple, yet complex factors. It involves two spouses who have a desire to win collectively versus being right individually. It takes a couple who desires to listen with compassion and speak words that are effective and sensitive to the other. The use of godly communication is a conscious choice, not a mandated behavior. So, the question is and will always be, what is your choice?

> *"Listen, open your ears, harness your desire to speak, and don't get worked up into a rage so easily, my brothers and sisters. Human anger is a futile exercise that will never produce God's kind of justice in this world."* (James 1:19-20, VOICE)

AT HIS PACE MINISTRIES
www.athispace.com

ARE YOU A
GOOD DEFENSIVE PLAYER?

RODNEY & NIKEYA YOUNG

Married ~ March 2009

Neither one of us have ever played sports, but we do enjoy watching a good game of football or basketball every now and then (Nikeya more so than Rodney, believe it or not). However, when it comes to our marriage, we are constantly striving to be "Defensive Player of the Year"! Why? Because our marriage is *valuable* to us, and when you have something that is highly valuable, what do you do? You *protect* it! During the COVID-19 pandemic, people all over the world were put on a collective "time out." We were forced to forego our busy lifestyles and get somewhere and sit down for a season. For some people, this season helped to bring their families closer together because families were collectively spending more time together than ever before. But for others, this season helped some couples decide to end their marriages because they were forced to spend more time together than ever before! I feel that for the latter, the reason for their split wasn't the pandemic, but a lack of playing good old-fashioned defense in their marriage. All the pandemic did was simply *expose* all of the poorly defended areas of the marriage.

Think about it… would you willingly leave your cell phone out, unlocked, on a table in a public area? Absolutely not! Too much important personal information is on that phone. Valuable access to precious parts of your life is on that phone, so you guard it with your life. Why do we spend more energy protecting our phones than we do for the most important relationship we have on earth? One reason is that we might not have gotten the memo: WE HAVE AN ACTIVE ENEMY seeking to destroy our marriages every day. :

> *"Be well-balanced (temperate, sober of mind), be vigilant and cautious at all times; for that enemy of yours, the devil, roams around like a lion roaring [in fierce hunger], seeking someone to seize upon and devour."* (1 Peter 5:8, AMPC)

We have been together for 15 years, and married for a little over 12 years now. Do we have a perfect relationship? No, because neither of us is perfect. However, we have a happy, strong, functional, godly relationship because we have defended it from the moment we entered into it! There are a number of things that we have done to defend our marriage, but some of the main ways we have defended it were through prayer, communicating/ spending quality time with one another, seeking accountability, and setting boundaries. In the courtship stages, we defended our relationship by praying together (either in person or over the phone) and having weekly meetings over coffee every Sunday after church. Sometimes, we studied the Bible during these meetings. Other times, we would bring a book on relationships, finances, or some other topic, and we would study that together. And then other times, we simply enjoyed one another's company. As simple as that sounds, we were setting the standards of communication early and often. Good communication skills are the foundation of any relationship. When you don't communicate with one another, you eventually start to grow apart without even realizing it.

One of the most important things we do is set boundaries. For instance, we don't allow others to come between us, whether it be friends, family members, or church members! We fiercely defend the unity in our marriage. An enemy of our spouse is an enemy of our covenant. This approach has repeatedly proven to save our marriage from damage from the outside forces! Another important boundary is that we don't spend time alone with members of the opposite sex. Call us old school, but many, many affairs have happened when someone spends lots of alone time with a work colleague! This has kept us out of a lot of compromising situations, and it is a strong point of trust we have with one another.

All in all, protect your marriage with your life! It is the most important relationship you have on earth, and God will empower your efforts to be the "Defensive Player of the Year" for your marriage!

www.nikeyayoung.com

JUST A REMINDER

R O B & N I C O L E W H E A T L E Y

Married ~ February 2012

God makes no mistakes—we are on this journey for a purpose. Marriages are not easy, but they are possible with an open heart and open mind. We have to learn to WORK it out.

ASSIGNMENTS

- You are not allowed to judge your spouse on what they write.
- Be intentional about making that happen.
- Talk about your rules for writing in the journal and your table of contents.

RECONNECT BEFORE THE SUNSET

GIOVANNI & SHAMIRA TATE

Married ~ June 2003

"'In your anger do not sin.' Do not let the sun go down while you are still angry." (Ephesians 4:26, NIV)

Displaying emotions is a part of our human nature. We often display love and happiness, but anger is one emotion that we will all experience in our marriage. The definition of anger is "a strong feeling of annoyance, displeasure or hostility," and it can arise at any moment.

When you first get married, you go through what they call the honeymoon phase. In this phase, no one can do any wrong; you both are on cloud nine, seeing eye to eye on everything, and living your best married life. You call each other pet name like "honey bear" and "love bug." Then suddenly one day someone gets angry, and you know that they are angry because instead of calling you their favorite pet name for you, they call you by your full government name. Then you, the other spouse who was not originally mad, get mad because they are mad. You then go from your daily routine of calling each other to just texting business transactions only, with no real connection for the entire day. One spouse is waiting for the other spouse to give in, but it is just not happening. The other spouse is tired of being the "I am sorry" spouse. Then you look up, and it is time to go to bed. You try to go to sleep, but it's super hot, then super cold, and then the covers cannot stay on you right and the pillows seem to have no fluff at all. You look up and see that your spouse is sleeping like a newborn baby, and now you are even angrier. So, there is no other choice but to pull an all-nighter and have heated fellowship, which is just conversation while angry, until you work it out and get back on cloud nine.

We are all human with human emotions, and at some point in our marriage, we will get mad or irritated, and yes, even angry. In your anger, do not sin. Do not name call or put each other down; do not add logs to the fire to create a bigger fire. Instead, take a minute to chill and calm down, pray or take a walk, or do something positive, then come back together and reconnect before the sunset.

Prayer:

> Lord, we know that anger is a normal emotion, but your Word says to be angry but sin not. When anger does arise, let us not destroy one another with our words or negative actions but help us to breathe, receive your peace, and recognize the traps of the enemy. Let us not forget your Word that teaches us that love endures. Help us to not go to bed angry, but help us to forgive as you have forgiven us. With you all things are possible, including working out our differences. In Jesus' name we pray.

Amen

1nessmarriage@gmail.com

LOVE. LISTEN. LEARN.

DUANE & TANYA REID

Married ~ December 1998

Today is another opportunity for us to release yesterday's thoughts about what could have, would have, and should have been. Instead of being stuck in our rearview mirrors, let's focus our hearts and heads on the beauty of *now*. Let's cherish the time we have to love our spouses, listen to our spouses, and learn about our spouses.

To love our spouses is a combination of showing it and saying it. Today, our focus is on saying it. How often do you say "I love you" to your spouse? And we mean really say it, like you did when you first fell in love with one another. The three words "I love you" have a tendency to get lost in marriage with the busyness of life—work, kids, volunteering, home maintenance, etc. In fact, "I love you" can get misused like "How are you?" It loses its authenticity and becomes automated. However, when we tell our spouses that we love them, we reaffirm our love for them and our marriage. Not saying "I love you" can create a disconnect that leads to unappreciation and unhappiness.

To listen to our spouses means seeking to understand, as opposed to seeking to be understood. We heard it put this way by Dr. Ben Thomason, and it has stuck with us: We have two ears. One ear is to hear what the person (in this case, our spouse) is saying, and the other ear is to hear what the person is not saying. For us, that means we have to shut off the "noise" around us and clearly tune in. We have to look at each other, listen attentively, ask questions, clarify answers, watch body language, etc. Listening to our spouses on the surface while not hearing (understanding) what they're really saying can lead to miscommunication, which has the great potential to breed frustration and ultimately division.

To learn about our spouses is a continual adventure. Our wants and needs evolve as we grow and mature. We can't assume that because our spouse was one way when we got married, they remain the same way. "I used to like you to rub my feet. Now I just want you to rub my lower back." As human beings, we are constantly changing. Our hobbies, habits, and hopes may have shifted, and that's okay. The key is that we commit to being life-long learners of our spouses, so that we are always learning and growing together.

Scripture:

"Whatever you have learned or received or heard from me, or seen in me—put it into practice. And the God of peace will be with you." (Philippians 4:9, NIV)

Prayer:

Father God, thank you for our marriage. Thank you for providing an example of selfless, sacrificial love. We understand that this type of love takes work, and we commit our marriage into your hands, as we commit to continually loving, listening to, and learning about one another. If we have done anything against you in thought, word, or deed, please forgive us. We ask for the fortitude, wisdom, discernment, network, and resources we need to build a beautiful, healthy, sustainable marriage. May joy, peace, laughter, and love fill our hearts and our home. In Jesus' Name, Amen.

themarriagereal@gmail.com
Social Media: @TheMarriageReal

FILL UP THE LOVE TANK

PATRICK & JESSICA PRICE

Married ~ July 1996

You must be a steward of your marriage the same way you would your bank account.

- Stewardship: the careful and responsible management of something entrusted to one's care

Make continual deposits into your marriage physically (physical touch or gifts), mentally (words of affirmation), spiritually (acts of service), and emotionally (quality time). Be intentional about making at least one of these deposits every day, even if it's a small amount, because it all adds to your bank account (marriage), and when you're a Kingdom citizen, the interest on your returns is unfathomable! Being a steward over anything requires frequent self-evaluations to ensure that your motives are correct. If you're not careful, your stewardship will turn into "Bad Management," which results in one of two disastrous situations: (1) you'll begin to sow just to get something in return, or (2) you'll begin to routinely withdraw from your bank account without ever replenishing it, which results in overdrafts (Proverbs 11:18).

Keep the Tank Filled (2 Chronicles 15:7)

Once you begin to get the stewardship in order, then you must do the maintenance necessary to maintain your marriage, the same way you would your car. Your spouse's love tank is like the gas tank of a car: just as driving a car depletes the gas, so do the years of building your marriage. Filling up your spouse's tank will require much SELFLESS LOVE and must be a heartfelt commitment—we made a commitment to keep God first!

Covenant love is what a person experiences as he/she enters relationship with God as God has ordained it. Therefore, when you're filling up your spouse car (your marriage), be sure to fill their spirit also, or it'll cause the engine to stall, likened to putting bad gas in your tank. You can fill up your marriage tank with prayer, compassion, and compromise... the healthy kind (1 Corinthians 3:6-7).

Remember, "good marriages" don't just happen, they're the product of hard work and continuous fill-ups! Here are a few things you can fill up your marriage with:

1. The Word instead of Worry
2. Prayer instead of Problems (selfishness)
3. Compassion instead of Confusion
4. Compromise instead of Complaint
5. Understanding instead of Utter Disappointment

Daily Secret Power

- Pray together and put God first for your life as individuals, and then as a married couple.

- Never shut down or shut out your spouse.

- Always say "I'm sorry," even if you are not wrong.

- Touch every day; physical touch is vital to a healthy marriage.

- Invest in your marriage; date always, vacation together.

- Seek out wise counsel; never hit a road that's too hard to turn around.

- Beware of distractions, even good ones.

- Priority is key! You are first in your world! God designed it that way.

Excerpt from SIMPLE SECRETS
Golden Nuggets from God's Word To Enhance your Marriage

YOUR HEART CAN HEAL

JOEY & MARILYN ALEXANDER

Married ~ September 1998

On February 12, my husband had open-heart surgery.

It was a little after 8 a.m. when they prepared to wheel him out of the room. We kissed and said, "See you in a few hours." I can still remember just how hard my heart was beating ... pounding. As I walked down the long corridor away from the prep room, I remember trying to shake the feelings of doubt and fear and trying to replace them with faith ... "Lord, YOU are the surgeon!"

I got to the door of the surgical waiting room and looked in the window. The room was dark; I was the first person there.

I pulled the door open, turned on the lights and sat down. I watched people come in after me, and soon the room was filled with conversations of others waiting for their loved ones to complete their surgery. About three hours later, the nurse who helped us in the prep room found me and said the surgery should be completed soon. Thank you, Jesus!

But just as I watched people come in after me, I watched those same people go out before me. And the longer the wait, the emptier the room, the louder the voices of doubt and fear became. The last person was called to recovery, and I was once again the only person in the room. Nine hours later . . . still waiting.

It was well after 5 p.m. when the surgeon opened the door. He touched me on the shoulder and smiled. I didn't even notice I was crying until I felt the teardrops on my hands. "He's on his way to ICU," he said. "The nurse will walk with you to the room." I could *not* stop crying! It was like the world had been lifted off my head and I could breathe again. As we walked to the ICU, the nurse tried to prepare me to see the many machines that would greet me. She held my hand and we walked up to the wide-open doors. She stood with me until I could compose myself. Nothing she said had prepared me to see him lying like that.

But God is so amazing!

Valentine's Day, two days after the surgery, I sat in the ICU again gripping his hand. A part of me was so relieved to be holding his hand again, and the other part of me was still overwhelmed, because even though they had removed some of the machines that God allowed to keep him alive, there were still so many left behind him.

But if you saw him now! Hallelujah! You. Would. Never. Know!

Now, seven months later, as we reflect on February, we are prompted to think about ALL of the couples who's marriages are also experiencing *heart failure*.

To you we say, "Please don't take each other for granted . . . stop bickering at the LITTLE stuff . . . AND the BIG stuff." All those things are so trivial when your spouse's heart is literally in someone else's hands. In life-or-death situations, you don't remember the arguments, you don't remember the attitudes, you don't remember the socks that are left on the floor . . . in those moments, ALL you think about is "Lord! Heal their heart so they can live!"

If your marriage is struggling through *heart failure*, there are people who are praying for you! "Father, help them get back to the same page. Help them to be the strength to their spouse's weakness. Help them to look at each other with the same eyes they had when they first met! Help them to see each other's heart."

God is able to heal (not just fix) every marriage. But it takes TWO—2—willing people to remember that they are not alone in this walk. When God touches your hearts, you both will grow and your marriage will live to flourish.

Lord, heal the heart of every marriage! Heal to break generational curses. Heal to overcome past bad decisions. Heal to break through past family scars. Heal so they will be an example to their children of how love should flow in a marriage.

If you allow Him, God can and will heal the hurt and the heart of your marriage so it will live to fulfill its destiny!

DESTINED TO PUBLISH
www.destinedtopublish.com

ROAD TRIPPIN'
BETTER TOGETHER

W E S   A N D   N E E S H A

Have you ever said to your spouse, "We are together because opposites attract"? After 32 years of marriage, we have come to realize that as much as we think we don't work well together sometimes, we truly complement each other in every way. There are definitely some areas we can improve in our communication, understanding, and even our intimate life, but there is no one else in this world designed better for me.

I've come to conclude that our differences are what make us stronger as a unit. Wesley is the type of person who appreciates structure, organization, and a plan, whereas Neesha is the type of person who flies by the seat of her pants and flourishes in the moment. We've discovered this is most obvious in our travel times. Neesha would love to take the scenic route, be adventurous, and go with no plan. Wesley, on the other hand, has a map and a plan before he gets in the car. He prefers a road trip to be mapped out from A to Z. This can be a struggle at times, but over the last 32 years, we can honestly say we have learned to adventure together, while acknowledging and respecting each other's strengths. It may be work to get there, but we rest on our foundation of love and realize being together is what makes the trip unforgettable.

We would like to encourage couples to know that it's okay to be different, and it's okay to have different ways of doing things. It is imperative that you make sure to learn how to travel this road of marriage together. Be willing to get in the driver's seat if your spouse is tired. Be open to bringing your ideas together to create a new traveling experience. What's most important is that you both stay in the car. Having different ideas, dreams, and visions is okay, as long as you have the same end goal in mind. Remain on one accord and embrace each other's differences, don't just tolerate them. After all, it will make the trip much more fun that way. Join us in meditating on this scripture where we find out how being together is God's idea, and together you and your spouse can accomplish so much more than if apart.

> *"Two are better than one, because they have a good return for their labor: If either of them falls down, one can help the other up. But pity anyone who falls and has no one to help them up. Also, if two lie down together, they will keep warm. But how can one keep warm alone? Though one may be overpowered, two can defend themselves. A cord of three strands is not quickly broken."* (Ecclesiastes 4:9-12, NIV)

YOUR PERSONAL
RELATIONSHIP

DOUG & SHANNA NEAL

Married ~ December 1996

YOUR PERSONAL CONNECTION: THE CATALYST OF FAITH TO GLORY

PASTOR SHANNA NEAL

"But when one turns to the Lord, the veil is removed. Now the Lord is the Spirit, and where the Spirit of the Lord is, there is freedom. And we all, with unveiled face, beholding the glory of the Lord, are being transformed into the same image from one degree of glory to another. For this comes from the Lord who is the Spirit." (2 Corinthians 3:16-18 ESV)

I can remember hearing the scripture and songs growing up about faith to faith and glory to glory, and "we are climbing Jacob's ladder," and "every round goes higher and higher." What this all meant was really beyond me once upon a time. Then, years ago now, I heard a teaching that involves growth and learning about God's growth process in His idea of the "life cycles within His creation". It took on an entire new meaning to me in my life of growth once I began to understand how relevant "the beginning of Creation" is to the way the Kingdom of God functions.

In the beginning of Creation, God created all living things to have a life cycle. In this life cycle, there are typically four stages: infancy, childhood, adolescence, and maturity or adulthood.

The stages are significant to proper development within a particular stage and a successful transition to the next stage of the life cycle. In the life cycle that God created, the first stage of infancy is all about dependency and survival. Like every infant needs to depend on someone else in order to thrive and survive, in our relationship with God, we must learn and adhere to this very same process of dependency in our development through infancy. The second stage of the life cycle is childhood, where we learn, grow, and develop through observation and exploration.

What I find most interesting is that we don't leave dependency behind us in the Kingdom of God and our relationship with God; it only increases as we take on the next stage in our life cycle of exploration, observation, and learning. As we are successfully growing into the third stage of adolescence, we now find ourselves feeling proud of what we've learned and accomplished. Through testing, we see our achievements and now are at risk of being a typical adolescent "know-it-all."

Just as we bring dependency with us from infancy to childhood, we also should bring the humility of observing, learning, listening to our adolescent stage. As we progress into the adulthood/maturity stage, it is another stage of all of the above processes working together, with one major difference: we now take on the biggest responsibility of proving our growth and development, and that is reproducing what the Creator has gifted us with in our process of growth. We are created beings with the gifts and capacity to create within us, to reproduce and bear much fruit in our lives.

What I really want to share that is most important to this process as believers in Christ is that we don't reach this finish line of maturity, but we continue to go to next levels, new heights, in a full-circle but higher-level continuum as we move forward in our relationship with God. One of the most practical ways we see this in our lives is through new careers and job opportunities. We start every new job in infancy, learning the people, the place, and all the new things we've never experienced before in this new situation. But as we adapt, observe, listen, grow, are tested, and achieve success in our submission to every stage of development, if we are faithful, promotion comes. Someone sees our growth, our faithfulness, and wants to advance us to another level of responsibility and/or authority. We begin to reproduce what we've received in helping to train the next person who comes into the job. We've reached maturation. But many get stuck in adolescence and worry about job security, pride and fear takes over, and they simply choose to only stay focused on themselves and not reproduce. For this reason, we have many adults (by age) stuck in adolescence (by stage). Whether in our marriages or family, or even in raising children, we can be sure that relationships are the ground in which God develops our growth. What better place to practice such submission to God's process of development?

This devotional is prefaced with a scripture from 2 Corinthians 3:16-18 that speaks of an "unveiled face." I truly believe that the true catalyst for all our growth into next places of faith and the marvelous glory of God begins with an unveiled face of receiving Jesus Christ as Lord first as our Savior and surrendering our life to Him and His purposes on the throne of our heart as our Sovereign. Only then can we truly begin the beautiful transforming cycles of faith to faith and glory to glory in His Kingdom.

WHEN CEILINGS BECOME FLOORS

DOUG NEAL

Many of us have either heard or used the phrase "Your ceiling will become your floor." We commonly hear this phrase in reference to breakthrough moments when God elevates us to a new level. What was once above us is now beneath us, bringing us to a brand-new place of authority in God's power. The old standard, which was good for its time, is now under our feet and a new place has sprung up before us. As God proclaims in Isaiah 43:19 (NKJV):

> *"Behold, I will do a new thing,*
> *Now it shall spring forth;*
> *Shall you not know it?*
> *I will even make a road in the wilderness*
> *And rivers in the desert."*

As believers in Christ, we have frequently and fittingly celebrated this verse with great fervor. The new things of God are worth celebrating when they spring up before us. But this verse also contains a question that we don't often address. It's the question, "Shall you not know it?"

New things are always exciting, even though they can sometimes be fraught with anxieties, like going to a new school, starting a new job, or moving to a new neighborhood. While new might be exciting, it also undeniably means change. And change usually means heading into the unknown.

What's also important to realize is that some of these new places of change don't always come about in the most favorable ways. Sometimes the new school is the result of failed classes. The new job can be the result of a layoff. And a new neighborhood can be the result of a prior eviction. But whether your new place comes as a result of promotion or just mere survival, it's important to keep in mind what Deuteronomy 31:8 (NIV) says:

> *"The Lord himself goes before you and will be with you;*
> *He will never leave you nor forsake you.*
> *Do not be afraid; do not be discouraged."*

Whatever new place God is bringing you to, remember that He has already gone ahead of you to prepare for your success. But everything new takes some getting used to, including the new places that God brings us to. Moving from one "floor" to the next can be challenging. If you think about breaking through the tiles, framework, and dry wall of an actual ceiling, you begin to realize that what's on the floor above is completely unseen and unfamiliar.

In 2009, our family moved from the suburbs of Chicago, IL, to a small town near South Bend, IN, to become campus pastors of a new church. We were breaking through our own ceiling, and we had a lot of adjusting to do. This role was somewhat like an associate pastor, just at a different location. Our young family was launched into a new and unknown place that sprang up before us without much warning. We accepted the challenge of leading a church of less than 80 people after having overseen a church campus of nearly 1,500 people.

Without question, it was difficult to adapt to this new place. We had many questions and sometimes doubts as to how the Lord was leading us. People around us didn't know whether to rejoice with us or feel sorry for us. We were still a part of the church that had sent us to South Bend, but both the spiritual and community cultures of these two vastly different environments often seemed to clash.

It wasn't long before a new ceiling needed to be broken through—the ceiling of becoming an independent church. This was not only new to us as ministry leaders, but it was also a role that neither my wife nor I really wanted. In fact, we had both determined a few years prior that we would be content to support whatever ministry the Lord sent us to and just leave it at that.

Nevertheless, the Lord had different plans for us. Twelve years later, we haven't exactly grown into a megachurch, but every week the atmosphere in our church is consistently saturated with the anointed presence of the Lord, filled with praise, adoration, and worship with the truth of God's Word being preached with love, power, and conviction. It has been a God-ordained journey that has greatly transformed our lives and richly blessed the lives of many people in our region.

Yet all of this took a great deal of patience and learning of what was initially unknown to us. Many of the changes our church has gone through have been very difficult to endure—changes in staff, new members coming, old members going, not to mention the financial challenges that come with running a much smaller church.

Obstacles like these always push us to trust God more and more. And each time we do, we see God move and not only sustain our church but cause us to thrive. We've seen steady growth in our membership and growth in our budget, but most importantly, we continue to see the spiritual growth and maturation of individuals and families as they faithfully serve the Lord.

Today, as we face the present state of our world together, we are globally undergoing the springing up of a new place. And whether this new place is the result of a promotion or just mere survival, the Lord our God goes before us. The present state of our world is no surprise to God. He will never leave nor forsake us. Therefore, we don't need to be afraid or discouraged. We can trust securely in the Lord to bring us through every test and trial that we face.

As we begin to adapt to our new surroundings, we will find challenges we've never faced, connect with people we've never related to, endure circumstances we've never encountered, do things we've never done, all to bring us to a new place we've never seen or known. It's at this point that we must make the decision whether to meet these challenges in our own strength or trust in the power and wisdom of the Lord.

New levels and next places always present exponentially growing challenges. For instance, transitioning between high school and college is much more demanding than moving from kindergarten to first grade. Moving from where you once were to where you are now undoubtedly had its challenges. But don't be surprised if where you're headed has an even greater degree of difficulty. Your new place will require an even greater intentional effort to press into God's presence and find help in time of need. As the Apostle Paul said in Philippians 3:13-14 (KJV):

> *"...forgetting those things which are behind,*
> *and reaching forth unto those things which are before,*
> *I press toward the mark for the prize*
> *of the high call of God in Christ Jesus."*

As you embark upon the journey to discover your new place, remember to trust God with all your heart and lean not on your own understanding. Our new places may be completely unfamiliar to us, and we may not know it as it springs up before us. But the Lord Himself has already gone before us. We can intentionally seek the Lord while He may be found and call upon Him while He is near. He will show us the path of life, and in His presence we will find the fullness of joy, and at His right hand pleasures forevermore as we embrace the new place that He is bringing us to.

CHRISTIAN LIFE CENTER SOUTH BEND
www.clcsb.org

Secret Spices for Intimacy

Thyme – Don't rush, take your THYME

Allspice – Make it an ALLSPICE night

Nutmeg – Add some NUTMEG to your apple pie

Cloves – Make sure your CLOVES are sexy

Cumin – Both spouses should achieve CUMIN

Fennel – It's too hot for FENNEL pajamas

Paprika – A little PAPRIKA might be fun

Poppy – Love it when you call him Big POPPY

Red Pepper – Never Crush the RED PEPPER.

Turmeric – It takes (two) TURMERIC for long-lasting love

Bonus Option: Excite your spouse with a little pop of Worcestershire BABY. (What this Here) You definitely will get CARAWAY!

Excerpt from SIMPLE SECRETS
Golden Nuggets from God's Word To Enhance your Marriage

Heart Life Connections

- HLM Recovery 180

- Crumbleknot Coaching

- Deborah C. Anthony

- My Bill Angel

- Mission Partners for Christ

- Destined To Publish

- Loved Well Boxes

- Oasis Empowerment

- Couples Committed to Becoming One

- iCan Dream Center

- Christian Life Center TP

- Christian Life Center SB

- The Tent Experience

CRUMBLEKN🪢T

BUILDING MARRIAGES AND FAMILIES THAT DON'T CRUMBLE.

Wes and Neesha are certified life, marriage, family, and relationship coaches. As relationship and marriage coaches, we work with a wide range of people and offer a highly personalized approach tailored to each individual.

In a supportive atmosphere, we help them attain the professional and personal growth they are striving for. We are grateful for the blessing to have seen thousands of marriages enriched and restored.

As Relationship Coaches, we specialize in the following areas:

- Strength Assessments
- Self-Repair
- Personal Growth
- Intimacy
- Professional Development
- Relationship Coaching
- Communication Skills
- Confidence & Personal Power
- Achieving Life Balance
- Health & Weight Issues
- Marketing & Network Consultant

Experience Leadership Certified Coach
John Maxwell Team Certified Coach
Prepare - Enrich Certified Counselor

www.Heartlifetoday.org | https://crumbleknot-coaching.square.site